Crochet
for Beginners
Step-by-step instructions and patterns

Consulting by Heidi Beazley

Written by Beth Taylor

Photo styling by Ewelina Rusek and Amy Stark

Photography by Christopher Hiltz, except pages 4, 5, 6, 67, and 101 from
Shutterstock.com and pages 5, 10, 57, and 70 from Getty

Crochet symbols and abbreviations from Craft Yarn Council's www.YarnStandards.com

Louis Weber, CEO
Publications International, Ltd.
8140 Lehigh Avenue
Morton Grove, IL 60053

Permission is never granted for commercial purposes.

ISBN: 978-1-64558-693-7

Manufactured in China.

8 7 6 5 4 3 2 1

Publications International, Ltd.

Table of Contents

Supplies

HOOKS, YARN & MATERIALS

What You'll Need

Crochet Hooks

Crochet hooks can be made from aluminum, plastic, wood, or bamboo. They are available in a wide range of sizes and are used with an assortment of yarns. Steel hooks are the smallest and are often used with fine thread in delicate crochet work, such as lace and doilies. Most patterns and yarn labels recommend a hook size. Select a crochet hook that feels comfortable to you and works well with your project and yarn.

Common Hook Sizes

U.S.	B-1	C-2	D-3	E-4	F-5	G-6	7	H-8	I-9	J-10	K-10.5	L-11	M-13	N-15	P	Q	S
mm	2.25	2.75	3.25	3.5	3.75	4	4.5	5	5.5	6	6.5	8	9	10	15	16	19

Needles

Tapestry or yarn needles have a blunt tip and an eye large enough to accommodate thick yarns. These special needles can be used to weave in yarn tails or sew crocheted pieces together.

Stitch Markers

As their name suggests, stitch markers are designed to mark your stitches. They can be used to mark a certain number of stitches, the beginning of a round, or where to make a particular stitch. Stitch markers must have openings so that they can be easily removed. You can purchase stitch markers, or improvise with pins, earrings, or safety pins.

Pins

Use long, rustproof pins for blocking and pinning seams together. Pins can also serve as stitch markers. Opt for pins with large, colorful heads that won't get lost in your crochet work.

Measurement Tools

Measuring tape is a must-have tool when taking body measurements before making garments. Measuring tape and rulers can be used to measure gauge.

All About Yarn

Yarn for Beginners

Before starting any new crochet project, you must select your yarn. For beginners learning the basic stitches, select a simple cotton yarn that is light colored, smooth, and sturdy. It's harder to see your stitches with dark colored yarn. Avoid fuzzy and loosely woven yarns that fray easily.

Yarn Fibers

Natural fibers

Cotton, linen, and hemp yarns are made from plant fibers. They are lightweight, breathable, and machine washable. Mercerized cotton has undergone a chemical process that results in stronger, shinier yarn.

Yarns made from animal fibers include wool, silk, cashmere, mohair, alpaca, and angora. These animal fibers are much warmer than plant fibers. Both types of natural fibers offer a bit of stretch.

Synthetic fibers

Yarns made from synthetic fibers include nylon, rayon, acrylic, and polyester. Synthetic yarns are usually less expensive than natural fibers, but are less breathable and pill more easily.

Novelty and specialty yarns

Novelty and specialty yarns can be tricky to work with, but create a distinctive look. They include bouclé, ladder, eyelash, and chenille. While great for trims and accessories, novelty yarn is not best for beginners.

Selecting Your Yarn

Each package of store-bought yarn has a label listing the yarn's length, fiber content, and weight. Yarn weight refers to the thickness of a yarn. It ranges from the thinnest embroidery thread to the bulkiest yarn. Yarn labels also recommend hook size—just look for the crochet hook symbol to find the U.S. and metric hook size.

Yarn Weight Guidelines

Yarn types: Fingering, lace, and 10-count crochet thread
Recommended hook sizes (metric): 1.5–2.25 mm
Recommended hook sizes (U.S.): Steel 6 to B-1
Crochet gauge range: 32–42 double crochet stitches to 4 in.

Yarn types: Sock, fingering, and baby
Recommended hook sizes (metric): 2.25–3.5 mm
Recommended hook sizes (U.S.): B-1 to E-4
Crochet gauge range: 21–32 single crochet stitches to 4 in.

Yarn types: Sport and baby
Recommended hook sizes (metric): 3.5–4.5 mm
Recommended hook sizes (U.S.): E-4 to 7
Crochet gauge range: 16–20 single crochet stitches to 4 in.

Yarn types: Double knitting and light worsted
Recommended hook sizes (metric): 4.5–5.5 mm
Recommended hook sizes (U.S.): 7 to I-9
Crochet gauge range: 12–17 single crochet stitches to 4 in.

Yarn types: Afghan, aran, and worsted
Recommended hook sizes (metric): 5.5–6.5 mm
Recommended hook sizes (U.S.): I-9 to K-10.5
Crochet gauge range: 11–14 single crochet stitches to 4 in.

Yarn types: Chunky, craft, and rug
Recommended hook sizes (metric): 6.5–9 mm
Recommended hook sizes (U.S.): K-10.5 to M-13
Crochet gauge range: 8–11 single crochet stitches to 4 in.

Yarn types: Bulky and roving
Recommended hook sizes (metric): 9–15 mm
Recommended hook sizes (U.S.): M-13 to Q
Crochet gauge range: 7–9 single crochet stitches to 4 in.

Yarn types: Jumbo and roving
Recommended hook sizes (metric): 15 mm and larger
Recommended hook sizes (U.S.): Q and larger
Crochet gauge range: 6 single crochet stitches and fewer to 4 in.

Source: Craft Yarn Council's www.YarnStandards.com

The Basics
GETTING STARTED

Holding the Hook

Pencil Hold

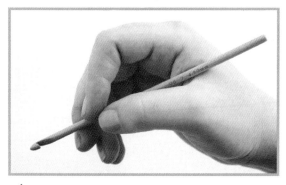

Knife Hold

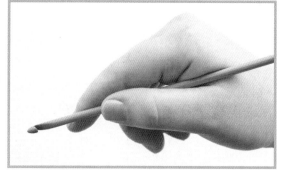

or

Tip: The instructions and photographs in this book are intended for right-handed crocheters. If you are a lefty, try holding up a mirror to the edge of a photograph to see the left-handed version.

Holding the Yarn

1

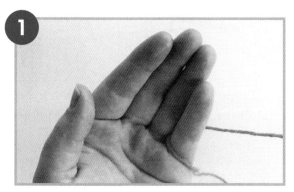

With your palm facing up, weave the working yarn (the yarn coming from the ball) between your pinky and ring fingers. Wrap the yarn clockwise around your pinky.

2

Take the yarn across your ring and middle fingers. Then wrap the yarn under and around your index finger.

3

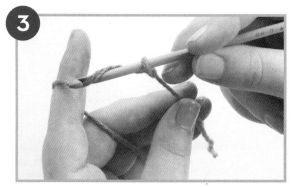

Hold the yarn under the slip knot with your left thumb and middle finger.

Tip: There are many ways to hold your yarn. Experiment with different methods until you find what is most comfortable for you.

Making a Slip Knot

The first step in any crochet project is a slip knot.
The slip knot is what attaches the yarn to your hook.

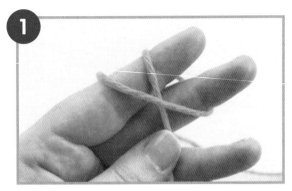

Wrap the yarn around your index and middle fingers on your yarn hand to create an X.

From the top, insert your hook under the first loop to grab the second loop.

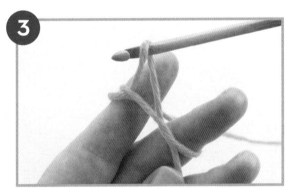

Draw the second loop you just grabbed under and up through the first loop.

Slide your fingers out. Pull your hook up while gently pulling both ends of the yarn down.

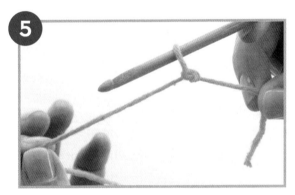

Pull the ends of the yarn to tighten the slip knot close to your hook.

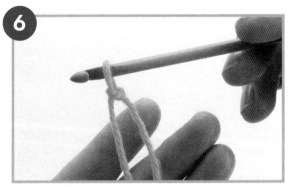

With a finished slip knot around your hook, you are ready to start crocheting.

Chain Stitch (ch)

Crochet often begins with a series of chain stitches used to make up the first row. This is called the foundation chain and is the basic start to most crochet projects.

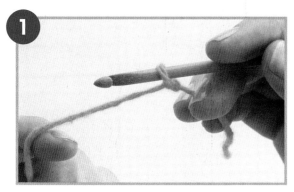

Start with a slip knot on your hook. Hold the yarn tail for tension.

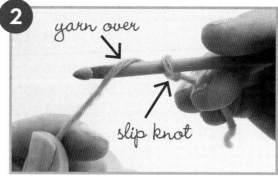

yarn over

slip knot

Bring the working yarn (the yarn coming from the ball) over your hook from back to front. This is called yarn over (yo).

Draw this section of yarn back through the slip knot. You will have 1 new loop on your hook when your first chain stitch is complete.

Yarn over again.

Draw this section of yarn through the loop on your hook. You will have 1 new loop on your hook each time you complete a chain stitch.

Repeat steps 2–3 until your foundation chain has the required number of chain stitches.

Counting Chains

Crochet patterns usually begin by telling you the number of chains needed for the foundation chain.

Identifying the Front and Back

The front of the foundation chain looks like a braid with a series of Vs. The back side of the foundation chain has a vertical ridge of bumps running down the middle from your hook to the end of the chain. Count chains from the front side.

Front

Back

Counting

Begin counting from the top of the foundation chain. (You can also count from the bottom up.) Do not count the loop on your hook or the slip knot on the bottom. Count only completed, V-shaped chain stitches. This example has 13 completed chain stitches.

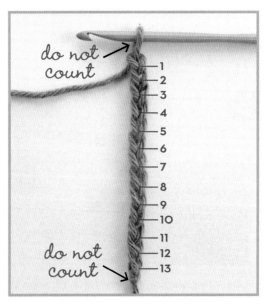

do not count

1
2
3
4
5
6
7
8
9
10
11
12
13

do not count

Tip: When creating a long foundation chain, it is helpful to use stitch markers every 10 or 20 stitches to make counting easier.

Turning Chains (tch)

Stitch	Number of Turning Chains
Slip stitch	0
Single crochet	1
Half double crochet	2
Double crochet	3
Treble crochet	4

Each crochet stitch requires a specific number of turning chains at the beginning or end of a row. The number of extra stitches needed for the turning chain is added to the number needed for the foundation chain.

Tension

Tension keeps your stitches neat and consistent. Make sure the chains in your foundation chain are even and loose enough to allow your hook back into those chains for the next row.

Too loose   **Too tight**   **Just right**

Slip Stitch (sl st)

The slip stitch is one of the most basic crochet stitches and is often used for joining.

1

Start with a foundation chain on your hook. Insert your hook from front to back into the second chain from your hook. There are 2 loops on your hook.

2

Yarn over, bringing the working yarn over your hook from back to front.

3

Draw the yarn through both loops on your hook. You will have 1 new loop on your hook when your first slip stitch is complete.

Single Crochet (sc)

How to single crochet:

To begin a row of single crochet, first stitch a foundation chain to the desired length. Add 1 extra chain stitch for the turning chain.

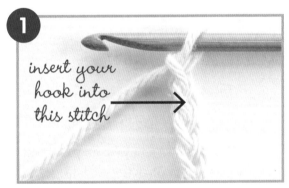

Insert your hook from front to back into the second chain stitch from your hook. There will now be 2 loops on your hook.

Yarn over. Draw this yarn through the first loop on your hook. There will be 2 loops on your hook.

3

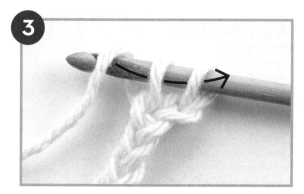

Yarn over again and draw this yarn through both loops on your hook. You will have 1 loop remaining on your hook when your first single crochet is complete.

4

insert your hook into this stitch

Insert your hook into the next chain stitch. Repeat steps 2–3 to complete another single crochet stitch.

5

Repeat step 4, working a single crochet stitch into each chain. At the end of the row, make 1 chain stitch for the turning chain.

6

insert your hook into this stitch

Turn your work so that the opposite side faces you. Insert your hook into the first single crochet stitch of the previous row and repeat steps 2–3. (Skip the turning chain.)

7

Insert your hook into the next stitch and repeat steps 2–3, working a single crochet stitch into each single crochet of the previous row.

8

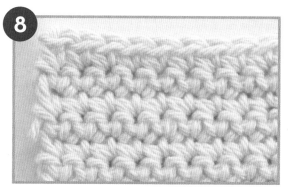

Repeat step 7 to continue the pattern. At the end of this and all subsequent rows, chain 1 for the turning chain and turn your work.

Half Double Crochet (hdc)

How to half double crochet:

To begin a row of half double crochet, first stitch a foundation chain to the desired length. Add 2 extra chain stitches for the turning chain.

insert your hook into this stitch

Yarn over. With this yarn over, insert your hook into the third chain stitch from your hook. There will be 3 loops on your hook.

Yarn over again. Draw the yarn through the first loop only. There will still be 3 loops on your hook.

3

Yarn over and draw the yarn through all 3 loops on your hook.

4

You will have 1 loop on your hook when your first half double crochet is complete.

5

insert your hook into this stitch

Yarn over. With this yarn over, insert your hook into the next chain stitch. There will be 3 loops on your hook. Repeat steps 2–4 to complete another half double crochet stitch.

6

Repeat step 5, working a half double crochet stitch into each chain stitch. At the end of the row, chain 2 for the turning chain.

7

insert your hook into this stitch

Turn your work so that the opposite side faces you. Yarn over and insert your hook into the second stitch. (The turning chain counts as the first half double crochet stitch in this row.) Repeat steps 2–4 to complete the half double crochet stitch.

8

Repeat step 5 to continue making half double crochet stitches into each stitch of the previous row. At the end of this and all subsequent rows, chain 2 for the turning chain and turn.

Double Crochet (dc)

How to double crochet:

To begin a row of double crochet, first stitch a foundation chain to the desired length.
Add 3 extra chain stitches for the turning chain.

insert your hook into this stitch

Yarn over. With this yarn over, insert your hook
into the fourth chain stitch from your hook.
There will be 3 loops on your hook.

Yarn over. Draw the yarn through the first
loop on your hook. There will be 3 loops on
your hook.

3

Yarn over. Draw the yarn through the first 2 loops on your hook only. There will now be 2 loops on your hook.

4

Yarn over again. Draw the yarn through the remaining 2 loops on your hook. You will have 1 loop on your hook when your first double crochet is complete.

5

insert your hook into this stitch

Yarn over. Insert your hook into the next chain stitch. Repeat steps 2–4 to complete another double crochet stitch.

6

Repeat step 5, working a double crochet stitch into each chain stitch. At the end of the row, chain 3 for the turning chain. Turn your work so that the opposite side faces you.

7

insert your hook into this stitch

Yarn over and insert your hook into the second stitch. (The turning chain counts as the first double crochet stitch in this row.) Repeat steps 2–4 to complete the double crochet stitch.

8

Repeat step 5 to continue making double crochet stitches into each stitch of the previous row. At the end of this and all subsequent rows, chain 3 for the turning chain and turn.

Treble Crochet (tr)

How to treble crochet:

To begin a row of treble crochet, first stitch a foundation chain to the desired length. Add 4 extra chain stitches for the turning chain.

Yarn over twice. Insert your hook into the fifth chain stitch from your hook. There will be 4 loops on your hook.

Yarn over once. Draw the yarn through the first loop on your hook. There will be 4 loops on your hook.

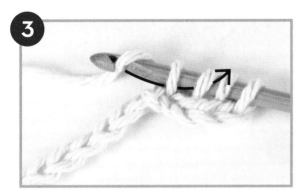

3 Yarn over once. Draw the yarn through the first 2 loops on your hook. There will be 3 loops on your hook.

4 Yarn over once. Draw the yarn through the first 2 loops on your hook again. There will be 2 loops on your hook.

5 Yarn over once. Draw the yarn through the remaining 2 loops on your hook. You will have 1 loop on your hook when your first treble crochet is complete.

insert your hook into this stitch

6 Yarn over twice and insert your hook into the next chain stitch. Repeat steps 2–5 to complete another treble crochet stitch.

insert your hook into this stitch

7 Repeat step 6, working a treble crochet stitch into each chain. At the end of the row, chain 4 for the turning chain. Turn your work so that the opposite side faces you. Yarn over twice and insert your hook into the second stitch. Repeat steps 2–5 to complete the treble crochet stitch.

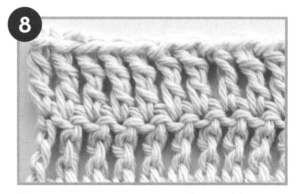

8 Repeat step 6 to continue making treble crochet stitches into each stitch of the previous row. At the end of this and all subsequent rows, chain 4 for the turning chain and turn.

Decreasing Stitches (dec)

To decrease within a row, combine multiple stitches together.

Single Crochet Decrease (sc2tog)

1 insert your hook into this stitch

Insert your hook into the next stitch as you would to start a single crochet.

2

Yarn over and draw the yarn through the stitch. There are now 2 loops on your hook.

3

Insert your hook into the next stitch. Yarn over and draw the yarn through the stitch. There are 3 loops on your hook.

4

Yarn over and draw the yarn through all 3 loops on your hook. You will have 1 loop on your hook when your first single crochet decrease (sc2tog) is complete.

Double Crochet Decrease (dc2tog)

1

Yarn over and insert your hook into the next stitch. Yarn over and draw the yarn through the stitch. Yarn over and draw the yarn through the first 2 loops. You will have 2 loops on your hook.

2

Yarn over and insert your hook into the next stitch. Yarn over and draw the yarn through the stitch. Yarn over and draw the yarn through the first 2 loops. You will have 3 loops on your hook.

3

Yarn over and draw the yarn through all 3 loops on your hook. You will have 1 loop on your hook when your first double crochet decrease (dc2tog) is complete.

Increasing Stitches (inc)

To increase within a row, work multiple stitches into the same stitch.

Single Crochet Increase (sc inc)

1

2

Insert your hook back into the same stitch you did your last single crochet in. Work another single crochet into that same stitch.

You will have 1 loop on your hook when your first single crochet increase is complete.

Double Crochet Increase (dc inc)

1

2

Insert your hook back into the same stitch in the previous row. Work another double crochet into that same stitch.

You will have 1 loop on your hook when your first double crochet increase is complete.

Front & Back Loops (FL & BL)

Working into the front or back loop only will create a unique texture and line.
These examples use half double crochet, but you can use these techniques with other stitches.

Tip: When your crochet work is in front of you, the front loop is the loop closer to you, while the back loop is farther from you.

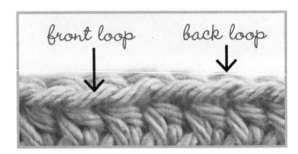

Front Loops

To work a half double crochet stitch into the front loop only (flo), yarn over and insert your hook into only the front loop closer to you. Complete the stitch as usual.

Continue working half double crochet stitches into only the front loops of the stitches in the previous row until you reach the end of the row. This creates a line.

Back Loops

To work a half double crochet stitch into the back loop only (blo), yarn over and insert your hook into only the back loop farther from you. Complete the stitch as usual.

Continue working half double crochet stitches into only the back loops of the stitches in the previous row until you reach the end of the row. This creates another line.

Working into Spaces

Some patterns will ask you to work into a space rather than a stitch of a previous row or round. This technique is demonstrated below using double crochet, but you can use other stitches.

Start at the position where you want to work into a space. Yarn over.

Insert your hook from front to back into the space (instead of the stitch). Yarn over and draw the yarn through the space.

Finish your double crochet as usual. You will have 1 loop on your hook when your first double crochet stitch into the space is complete.

Here is the row finished with double crochet stitches worked into the spaces.

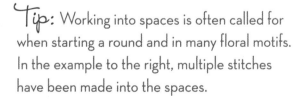

Tip: Working into spaces is often called for when starting a round and in many floral motifs. In the example to the right, multiple stitches have been made into the spaces.

Working in Rounds

To begin working in rounds, you have to first start with a center ring.
There are 2 different methods for starting a round, with a chain stitch ring or a magic circle.

Chain Stitch Ring

The chain stitch ring is made up of chain stitches that are joined together to form a ring. This method leaves a small opening in the center of your round.

Tip: Patterns will tell you how many chains to start with and what stitches to use. This example uses single crochet.

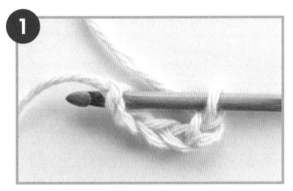

Chain 5 for a foundation chain. Insert your hook back into the first chain you made.

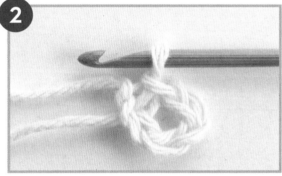

Work a slip stitch into that chain to form a ring.

Insert your hook into the center of the ring. Work a single crochet stitch into the ring.

Continue working single crochet stitches into the ring until you have made the required number of stitches. (For this example, 6 single crochet stitches.)

5

Work a slip stitch into the first single crochet you made to close up the ring.

6

You are now ready to start a round. (See page 29.)

Magic Circle

The magic circle forms a ring with your yarn that your first round of stitches are attached to. The ends are pulled to leave no opening in the center. That's the magic!

Tip: A chain stitch ring can replace a magic circle in a pattern.

1

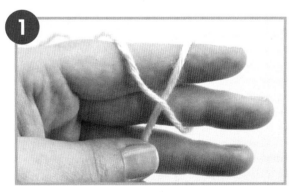

Loop the yarn around your fingers as shown to form an X.

2

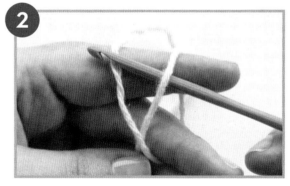

Take your hook under the bottom strand of the X. Use your hook to draw the other strand under the bottom strand. It will form a loose loop on your hook.

Remove the circle of yarn from your fingers. Yarn over. Draw the yarn through the loop on your hook. (This does not count as your first single crochet stitch.)

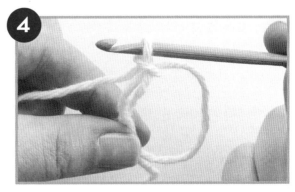

With your magic circle complete, you should now have a circle with the tail and the working yarn on the left side.

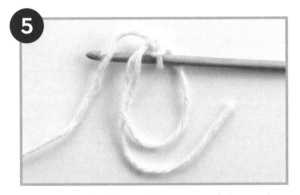

Insert your hook into the center of the circle. You are going to work a single crochet into that space. Yarn over and draw the yarn through the circle and tail. You will have 2 loops on your hook.

Yarn over again and draw the yarn through the remaining 2 loops on your hook. You will have 1 loop on your hook when your first single crochet stitch into the circle is complete.

Continue working the required number of single crochet stitches into the circle, making sure you are always working around the circle and the tail. If you run out of tail, pull it slightly. This closes the circle a little, but allows you to have a longer tail to work around.

When you have worked 6 single crochet stitches into the circle, pull the tail tightly to close the circle.

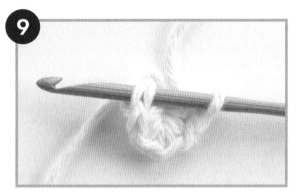

9 Insert your hook into the first single crochet stitch you made and make a slip stitch to close the circle.

10 With your slip stitch complete, you are now ready to start a round.

Starting a Round

To start a round, first begin by using either the chain stitch ring or magic circle method. This example used the magic circle method.

Round 1:

1 *insert your hook under these 2 loops* → Chain 1. Insert your hook under the top 2 loops of the first stitch and work a single crochet into that stitch.

2 Work 2 single crochets into each of the remaining stitches. (You will have 12 stitches.) Insert your hook back into the first stitch and make a slip stitch to close the round.

Rounds 2–6:

Each round increases by 6 stitches. The increases are evenly spaced in order to keep the circular shape. Close each round with a slip stitch back into the first stitch and then chain 1.

Round 2: Single crochet an increase in every other stitch for a total of 18 stitches.
Round 3: Single crochet an increase in every third stitch for a total of 24 stitches.
Round 4: Single crochet an increase in every fourth stitch for a total of 30 stitches.
Round 5: Single crochet an increase in every fifth stitch for a total of 36 stitches.
Round 6: Single crochet an increase in every sixth stitch for a total of 42 stitches.

For additional rounds, continue to evenly increase your rounds by 6 until your desired circumference.

Joining in New Yarn

At the End of a Row

To join in new yarn at the end of a row, work the last stitch with the old yarn until the final yarn over of the stitch. Yarn over with the new yarn.

Draw the new yarn through both loops on your hook. There is 1 loop on your hook. Continue stitching with the new yarn as usual.

In the Middle of a Row

To join in new yarn in the middle of a row, work the last stitch with the old yarn until the final yarn over of the stitch. Yarn over with the new yarn.

Draw the new yarn through both loops on your hook. There is 1 loop on your hook. Continue stitching with the new yarn as usual until you reach the end of the row.

Tip: Rather than leaving the tail of the old yarn in the middle of the row, you can work over the old yarn until you reach the end of the row. You can then weave in all yarn tails at the edges later.

Fastening Off

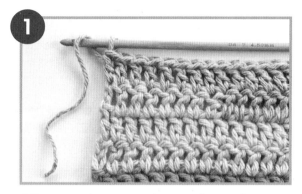

After completing your last stitch, cut the excess yarn, leaving several inches to weave the tail in later. Yarn over and draw the yarn tail through the loop on your hook.

Pull the yarn tail to tighten.

Weaving in the Tail

Thread one of your yarn tails into a blunt-tipped needle. Insert the needle into the first stitch and draw the yarn through.

Continue weaving the needle under and over the stitches around the edge.

Cut the yarn close to the final stitch when you're done weaving in the tail.

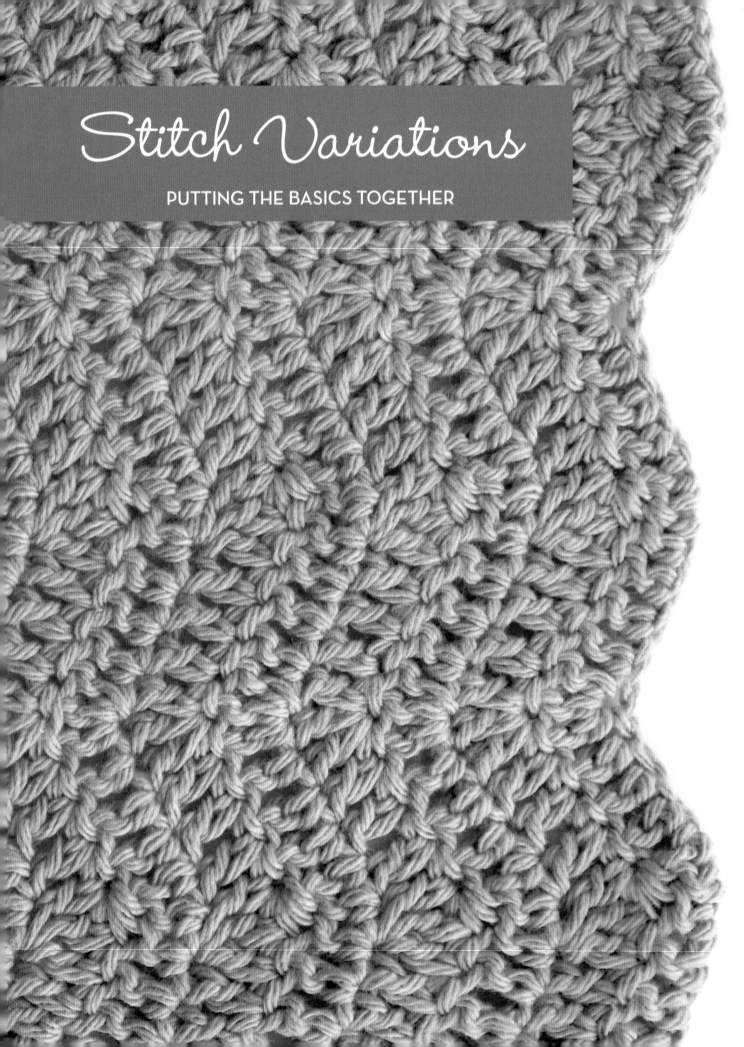

Stitch Variations

PUTTING THE BASICS TOGETHER

Basketweave

This basketweave uses alternating front post double crochet (FPdc) and back post double crochet (BPdc) stitches. Post stitches are sometimes called raised stitches.

Start with a foundation chain that has a multiple of 6 chains, plus 4.

Front & Back Posts:

Instead of inserting your hook into a stitch or space, you insert it around the front or back of a post. The stitches are worked the same as usual. The only difference is where your hook is inserted.

Front Posts:
Insert your hook under the post from the front side.

Back Posts:
Insert your hook under the post from the back side.

Row 1:

1 In the 4th chain from your hook, work 1 double crochet. Continue across the row, working 1 double crochet into each chain.

2 Chain 2 for the turning chain and turn your work so that the opposite side faces you.

Row 2:

Work 1 double crochet around the 2nd front post of the previous row (FPdc). To do this, yarn over (because you are doing a double crochet) and insert your hook under the 2nd post. Finish your double crochet stitch as usual.

Work a FPdc stitch into the next 2 posts so there are a total of 3.

Work 1 double crochet around the next back post (BPdc). To do this, yarn over (because you are doing a double crochet) and insert your hook, from the back side, under the next post. Finish your double crochet stitch as usual.

Work a BPdc stitch into the next 2 posts so there are a total of 3.

Continue across the row, alternating 3 FPdc stitches with 3 BPdc stitches. Finish the row by working 1 double crochet into the top chain of the turning chain.

Chain 2 for the turning chain and turn your work so that the opposite side faces you.

Row 3:

Repeat row 2, alternating 3 FPdc stitches with 3 BPdc stitches across the row. Work 1 double crochet into the top of the turning chain. Chain 2 and turn.

Row 4:

Work 1 BPdc stitch around the 2nd post. Work 1 BPdc stitch around the next 2 posts for a total of 3 BPdc stitches.

Work 3 FPdc stitches around the next 3 posts. Continue across the row, alternating 3 BPdc stitches with 3 FPdc stitches.

3. Work 1 double crochet into the top of the last turning chain.

4. Chain 2 for the turning chain and turn your work so that the opposite side faces you.

Row 5:

1. Repeat row 4, alternating 3 BPdc stitches with 3 FPdc stitches across the row. Work 1 double crochet into the top of the turning chain. Chain 2 and turn.

Repeat rows 2–5 to continue the pattern.

Popcorns (pc)

The popcorn stitch works several stitches into the same space, resulting in a "puffed" pattern and texture.

To make a popcorn using single and double crochet, start with a foundation chain that has a multiple of 3 chain stitches.

Row 1:

Work 1 single crochet into the second chain from your hook.

Finish the row with single crochet stitches. Chain 1 for the turning chain.

Row 2:

Turn your work so the opposite side faces you. Work a single crochet into each of the next 2 stitches.

In the next stitch, work 5 double crochets into the same stitch. Drop the loop you created by removing your hook.

Insert your hook under the top 2 loops of the first double crochet of the group.

Grab the dropped loop with your hook and draw the yarn through the stitch. Add a chain stitch to complete your first popcorn stitch. You will have 1 loop on your hook.

Work 1 single crochet into each of the next 3 stitches.

Continue to the end of the row, alternating between the popcorn stitch and the single crochet stitches. At the end of row, chain 1 for the turning chain.

Row 3:

Turn your work so the opposite side faces you. Work 1 single crochet stitch into each stitch across the row.

Tip: For rows of staggered popcorn stitches like in our example swatch, reduce the number of single crochet stitches at the beginning of every other popcorn row. Then complete the popcorn rows as usual.

Repeat rows 2–3 to continue the pattern.

V-Stitch

The V-stitch makes a series of interlocking Vs. This stitch works up quickly and is great for making afghans.

To make V-stitches using double crochet, start with a foundation chain that has a multiple of 3 chains, plus 7.

Row 1:

1 Work 1 double crochet into the fourth chain from your hook. Chain 1.

2 Skip 1 chain stitch and work 1 double crochet into the next chain. Chain 1.

3 Work 1 double crochet into the very same chain. You will have 1 loop on your hook when your first V-stitch is complete.

4 Skip 2 chains and work 1 double crochet into the next chain. Chain 1. Work 1 double crochet into the very same stitch.

5

Repeat step 4 across the row until you have 4 chains left. Chain 1.

6

Skip 2 chains. Work 1 double crochet into each of the last 2 chains to end the row.

7

At the end of the row, chain 3 for the turning chain. Turn your work so the opposite side faces you.

Tip: A chain-1 space is the space created by the chain 1 between the 2 double crochet stitches. It looks like the center of a V.

this is a chain-1 space

Row 2:

1

The turning chain counts as the first double crochet in this row. Work 1 double crochet into the next stitch and chain 1.

2

Work 1 V-stitch into each chain-1 space (center of each V) across the row until you have 1 chain space and 2 double crochet stitches left.

3 When you have 1 chain space and 2 double crochet stitches left, chain 1 and skip the chain-1 space. Work 1 double crochet into each of the last 2 double crochet stitches to end the row. Chain 3 for the turning chain and turn.

Repeat row 2 to continue the pattern.

Shell Stitch

Shells are created by working several stitches into the same stitch or space. They are also called fan stitches.

To make shell stitches using single and double crochet, start with a foundation chain that has a multiple of 4 chains, plus 1.

Row 1:

In the fifth chain from your hook, work 4 double crochet stitches.

Skip the next 3 chains and work 4 double crochet stitches into the next chain.

Repeat step 2 across the row until there are 4 chains left. Skip 3 chains and work 2 double crochet stitches into the last chain. Chain 1 for the turning chain and turn your work so that the opposite side faces you.

Row 2:

Work 1 single crochet into each of the double crochet stitches from the previous row. Chain 3 for the turning chain and turn your work so that the opposite side faces you.

Row 3:

1. Work 1 double crochet into the first stitch. Skip 3 stitches.

2. Work 4 double crochets into the next single crochet stitch. Skip the next 3 single crochet stitches.

3. Repeat step 2 across the row until there are 2 stitches left.

4. Skip the next single crochet stitch and work 1 double crochet into the last stitch.

5. Chain 1 for the turning chain and turn your work so that the opposite side faces you.

Row 4:

1. Work 1 single crochet into the next double crochet.

2. Continue working 1 single crochet into each double crochet stitch across the row.

3. Work 1 single crochet stitch into the top of the turning chain from the previous row.

4. Chain 3 for the turning chain and turn your work so that the opposite side faces you.

Row 5:

1. Skip the first 2 single crochet stitches.

2. Work 4 double crochet stitches into the next single crochet.

3. Skip the next 3 single crochets.

4. Repeat steps 2–3 across the row until there are 2 stitches left.

5. Skip the next stitch and work 1 double crochet stitch into the last stitch of the previous row.

6. Chain 1 for the turning chain and turn your work so that the opposite side faces you.

Repeat rows 4–5 to continue the pattern.

Bobbles (bo)

Bobbles work multiple stitches together into 1 stitch or space.

This bobble uses single and double crochet. Start with a foundation chain that has any odd number of chains.

Row 1:

1 In the 2nd chain from your hook, work 1 single crochet stitch.

2 Chain 1. Skip 1 chain and work 1 single crochet stitch into the next chain. Repeat step 2 across the row.

3 At the end of the row, chain 3 for the turning chain and turn your work so that the opposite side faces you.

Row 2:

1 Skip the first stitch. (The turning chain counts as the first double crochet in this row.)

Row 2 (continued):

In the next chain space, double crochet 5 together (dc5tog) following the tip instructions.

Tip: **How to double crochet 5 together:**

1. Yarn over. Insert your hook into the chain space.

2. Yarn over and draw the yarn through the space.

3. Yarn over and draw the yarn through the first 2 loops on your hook.

4. Repeat steps 1–3, inserting your hook into the same chain space, until you have 6 loops on your hook. Each time you repeat this process, you will add another loop to your hook.

On your final bobble, yarn over and draw the yarn through all 6 loops on your hook. (You will have 1 loop on your hook when your 5 double crochets are complete.)

Make 1 chain stitch to secure and complete the bobble.

Repeat steps 2–4 across the row, ending with 1 double crochet in the last single crochet of the row. Chain 1 for the turning chain and turn your work.

Row 3:

1. Work 1 single crochet into the first stitch.

2. Chain 1. Skip 1 chain and work 1 single crochet into the next stitch.

3. Repeat step 2 across the row.

Repeat rows 2–3 to continue the pattern.

Clusters (CL)

You make clusters by combining stitches together into the same stitch or space.

To make cluster stitches using single crochet, start with a foundation chain that has a multiple of 2 chains, plus 1.

Tip: **How to single crochet 2 together using 2 chain spaces:**

1. Insert your hook into the chain space to be worked.

2. Yarn over and draw the yarn through the space. You will have 2 loops on your hook.

3. Insert your hook into the next chain space.

4. Yarn over and draw the yarn through the space. There will be 3 loops on your hook.

5. Yarn over and draw the yarn through all 3 loops on your hook. There will be 1 loop left on your hook.

these are the chain spaces

Row 1:

In the second chain from your hook, work 1 single crochet stitch.

Chain 1. Skip 1 chain and work 1 single crochet into the next chain. Repeat step 2 across the row. Chain 1 for the turning chain.

Row 2:

1

Turn your work so that the opposite side faces you. Work 1 single crochet into the first stitch of the row. Chain 1.

2

Following the tip instructions, single crochet 2 together (sc2tog), working into the next 2 chain spaces. Chain 1 when you're finished.

3

work back into this chain space

Insert your hook back into the chain space you just worked in. Single crochet 2 together using this chain space and the next. Chain 1.

4

Repeat step 3 across the row, ending the row with 1 single crochet in the last stitch. Chain 1 for the turning chain and turn your work so that the opposite side faces you.

Row 3:

1. Work 1 single crochet into the first stitch.

2. Chain 1.

3. Skip 1 chain and work 1 single crochet into the next stitch.

4. Repeat steps 2–3 across the row.

Repeat rows 2–3 to continue the pattern.

Finishing Techniques

Edging Techniques

There are many different edging techniques, which can be crocheted or sewn.
Each technique will give your piece a finished and unique look. Here are a few examples.

Shell Stitch Edge

The shells in this example are made from 5 double crochet stitches into the same single crochet stitch. Start with a row of single crochet around the edge of your piece.

1 Insert your hook into the single crochet stitch in the upper right-hand corner and secure the yarn with a slip stitch. Chain 3.

2 In the next stitch, work 2 double crochets.

3 Chain 1. Skip 1 stitch and work 1 single crochet into the next stitch.

4 Chain 1. Skip 1 stitch and work 5 double crochets into the next stitch. Your first 5-dc shell is complete.

5 Repeat steps 2–4 around your entire piece. End with 3 more double crochets in the same stitch into which you worked the 2 double crochets in step 2 to complete the 5-dc shell.

Picot Stitch Edge

Picot edges can either be made small or large. They can be worked into stitches or spaces and can be added to any row of stitches. Here picots are added to rows of single crochet.

Small picot

Large picot

Small Picot

Insert your hook anywhere along the edge and join your edging yarn with a slip stitch.

Chain 3. Insert your hook into the third chain from your hook. Yarn over and draw the yarn through both loops to complete 1 small picot.

Work 1 single crochet into each of the next 3 stitches.

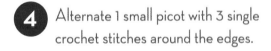 Alternate 1 small picot with 3 single crochet stitches around the edges.

Large Picot

1. Insert your hook anywhere along the edge and join your edging yarn with a slip stitch.

2. Chain 5. Insert your hook into the fifth chain from your hook. Yarn over and draw the yarn through both loops to complete 1 large picot.

3. Work 1 single crochet into each of the next 3 stitches.

4. Alternate 1 large picot with 3 single crochet stitches around the edges.

Crab Stitch Edge

Crab stitch is also called reverse single crochet.
Start with a row of single crochet along the edge.

1 Secure the new yarn with a slip stitch in the top left-hand corner.

2 Insert your hook into the same stitch you just worked into.

3 Yarn over and draw the yarn through the stitch (the first loop on your hook). There are 2 loops on your hook.

4 Yarn over again and draw the yarn through both loops on your hook. You will have 1 loop on your hook when your first crab stitch is complete.

5 Repeat steps 2–4 across the edge, working 1 crab stitch into each single crochet to the right.

Tip: To continue the edging around a corner, work multiple crab stitches into the same corner stitch.

Blanket Stitch Edge

The blanket stitch is sewn rather than crocheted. It lies flat and can help disguise uneven edges.

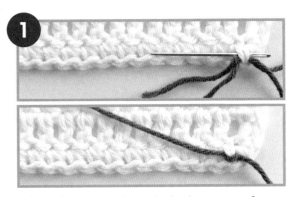

1 Thread the yarn through the large eye of a tapestry needle. With the wrong side facing up, secure the yarn to the bottom right-hand side of the crochet piece.

2 Flip the crochet piece so the right side is facing up. Draw the needle from back to front through the bottom left-hand side.

3 Insert the needle from front to back through the next small space on the edge.

4 Pull the needle through, going over the loop that was created. You have completed 1 blanket stitch.

5 Continue across the edge, working blanket stitches into the spaces between stitches.

Tip: To continue the edging around a corner, work multiple blanket stitches into the same corner space.

Joining Pieces Together

There are many techniques for joining pieces together, including both crochet and sewing methods. Some methods create a bulkier seam and will be sturdier. Other methods are less bulky, but might be more delicate. Use the same yarn from your project to help disguise the seams. Using a different color yarn makes seams more obvious, but can add more detail to your project.

Single Crochet Join

To join crochet pieces together with single crochet, start by placing the pieces with right sides together and stitches or rows lined up.

Tip: The only difference between a regular row of single crochet stitches and a single crochet join is that you will be working each stitch in both pieces.

Front side

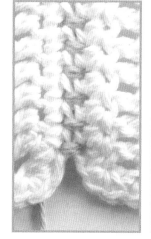

Back side

1

Insert your hook from front to back under the first pair of stitches on both pieces. Make a slip knot and attach it to the end of your hook.

2

Draw the slip knot through both pieces, letting the knot catch on the back. Yarn over and draw through the loop on your hook. Yarn over again and draw through both loops on your hook.

3 Insert your hook from front to back under the next pair of stitches and work a single crochet stitch.

4 Repeat step 3 across the seam, working 1 single crochet in each pair of stitches. When complete, fasten off and weave in yarn tails.

Slip Stitch Join

To join crochet pieces with slip stitch, start by placing the pieces with right sides together and stitches or rows lined up.

Tip: To make the slip stitch seam less bulky, try only working through 1 loop of each stitch.

Front side   **Back side**

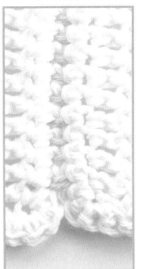 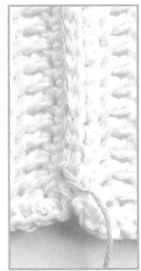

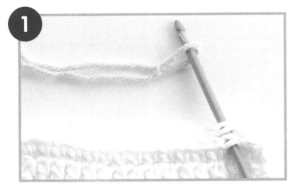

1 Insert your hook from front to back under the first corresponding pair of stitches of both pieces on the right. Make a slip knot and attach it to the end of your hook.

2 Draw the slip knot through both pieces. The knot will catch on the back. Yarn over and draw the yarn through the loop on your hook.

3 Insert your hook from front to back under the next pair of corresponding stitches on the left. Yarn over and draw the yarn through both loops on your hook. You will have 1 loop on your hook when your first slip stitch is complete.

4 Repeat step 3 across the seam. When complete, fasten off and weave in yarn tails.

Backstitch Join

The backstitch is a sewing method you can use to join crochet pieces together. It is extra strong, but bulky.

To join 2 crochet pieces with backstitch, start by placing the pieces with right sides together and stitches or rows lined up. Cut a piece of matching yarn to sew with. A piece too long will be difficult to work with.

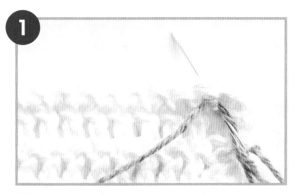

1 Using a threaded tapestry needle, secure the yarn close to the top right edge. Insert the needle from front to back through both pieces in the first stitch.

2 From back to front, bring the needle through the next stitch on the left. Draw the yarn through. From front to back, insert the needle into the first stitch and draw through.

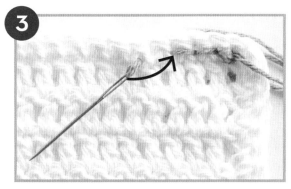

3 Skip the first stitch on the left. From back to front, bring the needle through the next stitch. Draw the yarn through. From front to back, insert the needle into the previous stitch and draw through.

4 Repeat step 3 across the seam. When complete, fasten off and weave in the yarn tails.

 Tip: Match the size of your backstitches to the size of the crochet stitches in your project.

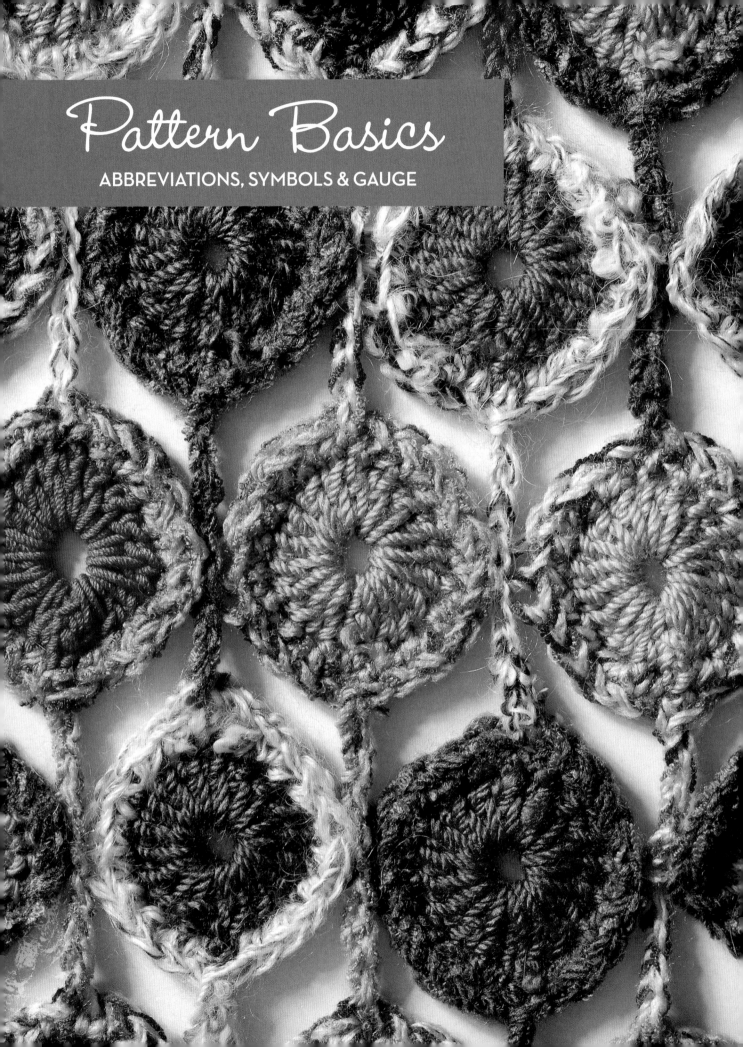

Pattern Basics

ABBREVIATIONS, SYMBOLS & GAUGE

Abbreviations & Symbols

Crochet patterns often use abbreviations and symbols as shorthand to represent frequently used stitches and techniques. Use the guide below as you start to follow patterns using shorthand.

Abbreviations

alt	alternate
approx	approximately
beg	begin/beginning
bet	between
BL or blo	back loop or back loop only
bo	bobble
BP	back post
BPdc	back post double crochet
BPhdc	back post half double crochet
BPsc	back post single crochet
BPtr	back post treble crochet
CC	contrasting color
ch	chain(s)
ch-sp	chain space(s)
CL	cluster
cm	centimeter(s)
cont	continue
dc	double crochet(s)
dec	decrease(s)/decreasing
dtr	double treble crochet(s)
FL or flo	front loop or front loop only
FP	front post
FPdc	front post double crochet
FPhdc	front post half double crochet
FPsc	front post single crochet
FPtr	front post treble crochet
hdc	half double crochet(s)
hk	hook
inc	increase(s)/increasing
lp(s)	loop(s)
MC	main color
mm	millimeter(s)

p	picot
pc	popcorn
pat(s)	pattern(s)
pm	place marker
prev	previous
rem	remain/remaining
rep	repeat(s)
rnd(s)	round(s)
RS	right side
sc	single crochet(s)
sl st	slip stitch
sk	skip
sp(s)	space(s)
st(s)	stitch(es)
tch	turning chain(s)
tog	together
tr	treble crochet(s)
WS	wrong side
yd(s)	yard(s)
yo	yarn over
" or in	inch(es)
[ ]	work instructions within brackets as many times as directed
( )	work instructions within parentheses as many times as directed
*	repeat the instructions following the single asterisk as directed
**	repeat the instructions between asterisks as many times as directed or repeat from a given set of instructions

Symbols

⌒	chain
•	slip stitch
X or †	single crochet
	half double crochet
	double crochet
	treble crochet
	sc2tog
	sc3tog
	dc2tog
	dc3tog
	3-dc cluster
	3-hdc cluster/ puff st/bobble
	5-dc popcorn
	5-dc shell
	ch-3 picot
	front post dc
	back post dc
⌒	worked in back loop only**
⌣	worked in front loop only**

**Symbol appears at base of stitch being worked

Gauge

Gauge refers to how many stitches and rows you should have in a given area in order to match the measurements of a project. The pattern will state how many stitches and rows are needed to achieve the proper gauge. For the projects in this book, gauge is not important. It's most important when making clothing items, like sweaters or socks, in order to get the proper fit.

Four things determine your gauge:

- Tension (how loosely or tightly you form the stitches)
- Type and weight of the yarn
- Size of the hook
- Stitch being worked

Making your gauge swatch

Using the same yarn, hook size, and stitch you plan to use for the pattern, crochet a swatch at least 4 x 4 inches. If the project has specific gauge instructions, follow those. After your gauge swatch is complete, lay it on a flat surface.

Measuring your gauge swatch

Use a ruler, measuring tape, or gauge tool and measure 4 inches across your swatch and mark it with pins. Count the number of stitches between the pins. This is your stitch gauge.

Next you will need to measure the row gauge. Place your measuring tool vertically on the swatch, measure 4 inches, and mark it with pins. Count the number of rows between the pins. This is your row gauge.

Adjusting your gauge

If your gauge swatch has too many stitches or rows compared to the pattern, use a larger hook. If your gauge swatch doesn't have enough stitches or rows, use a smaller hook. Keep adjusting your hook size until you have the required gauge.

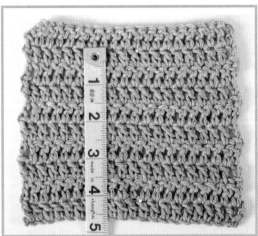

Tip: The stitch gauge is more important than the row gauge. That's because it is easier to adjust the number of rows than to adjust the number of stitches in your crochet project.

Crochet Patterns

Tip: The long edge of the completed triangle shawl is about 42" and the shorter edges are about 33" long. The shawl measures 27" from the middle of the long edge down to the point.

Triangle Shawl with Tassels

Skill Level

BEGINNER

Materials

 1 skein (590 yards) for shawl, 20 yards scrap yarn for tassels

Hook: 5 mm/U.S. H-8

Other: Large tassel maker, scissors, tapestry needle

Stitches Used

Chain stitch (ch)

Double crochet (dc)

Single crochet (sc)

Instructions

Ch 3.

Row 1: Skip the first 2 ch, 2 dc, ch 2, 3 sc in last ch st.

Row 2: Ch 2, turn. Dc in same st as ch 2, dc in next 2 sts, (2 dc, ch 2, 2 dc) in ch-2 sp, dc in next 2 sts, 2 dc in last st.

Row 3: Ch 2, turn. Dc in same st as ch 2, dc in each dc st to ch-2 sp, (2 dc, ch 2, 2 dc) in ch-2 sp, dc in each st to last st, 2 dc in last st.

Rows 4–7: Repeat row 3.

Rows 8–12: Ch 2, turn. Dc in same st as ch 2, dc in each dc st to ch-2 sp, (2 dc, ch 2, 2 dc) in ch-2 sp, dc in each st to last st, 2 dc in last st.

Row 13: Ch 2, turn. Dc in same st as ch 2. *Ch 1, skip 1 st, 1 dc; repeat from * to ch-2 sp. Ch 1, (2 dc, ch 2, 2 dc) in ch-2 sp. **Ch 1, skip 1 st, dc; repeat from ** to end of row. Ch 1, skip 1 st, 2 sc in last st.

Rows 14–41: Repeat rows 8–13.

Fasten off and weave in yarn tails.

Tassels (make 2)

The shawl will likely use all 590 yards of yarn, so you'll need additional yarn to make the tassels. Each tassel on this shawl is made with 10-yard scraps of 4/medium yarn, but you can use any yarn weight—just adjust the number of wraps to compensate for thicker or thinner yarn.

Step 1: Adjust large tassel maker to desired height from the front side. Flip to back side of tassel maker and tuck yarn tail into the notch on one side as shown below.

Step 2: Wrap yarn around the tassel maker 15 times; the more wraps, the thicker the tassel. Tuck the end of the yarn into the notch on the other side of the tassel maker.

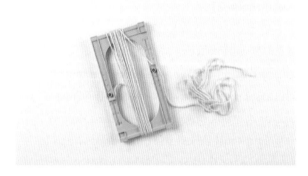

Step 3: Trim yarn end. Cut 2 lengths of yarn—one about 12" long, the other about 8" long.

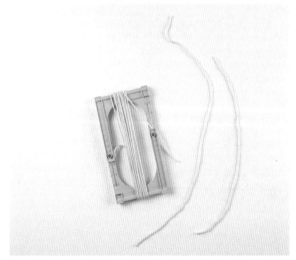

Step 4: Place the 12" length of yarn under the vertical wraps of yarn.

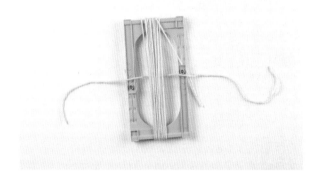

Step 5: Tie 2 tight knots in the front side facing up—the tighter the better.

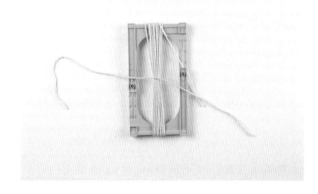

Step 6: Place scissors in the groove at the top of the tassel maker frame and cut wrapped strands of yarn.

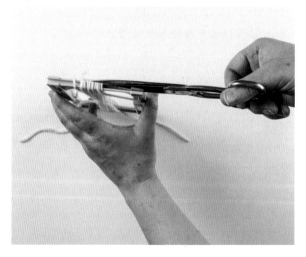

Tip: You can also use a piece of cardboard or a book to create your own tassel maker.

Step 7: Turn tassel maker frame over, place scissors in groove, and cut wrapped strands of yarn to remove tassel. Below is the tassel completely removed from the frame.

Step 8: Fold the top half of the tassel down. Pull the 2 long ends from the knots you tied in the middle up to the top. You will use these to attach the tassel to the shawl later.

Step 9: Place the 8" length of yarn under the top of the tassel as shown. This will form the head.

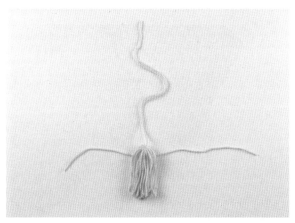

Step 10: Tie a knot on this side.

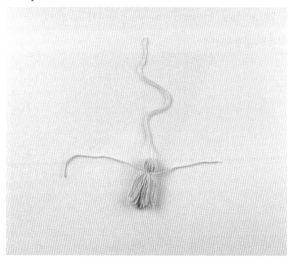

Step 11: Wrap the yarn around and tie another knot on the other side.

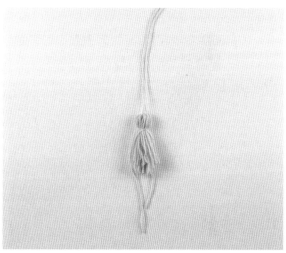

Step 12: Take tassel in hand as shown below and trim tassel ends to neaten.

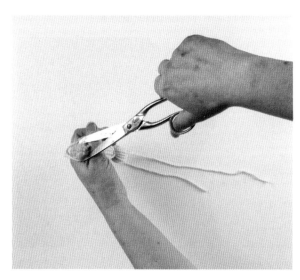

Step 13: Find corner of shawl where tassel will be attached. Thread one yarn tail through a tapestry needle.

Step 14: Insert the threaded tapestry needle up through a corner stitch.

Step 15: Draw yarn through. Thread the other yarn tail through a tapestry needle.

Step 16: Insert threaded tapestry needle through another nearby corner stitch (do not use same corner stitch as step 14). Draw yarn through.

Step 17: Tie a double knot with the 2 yarn tails.

Step 18: Insert needle threaded with yarn tail into top of tassel head. Repeat with other yarn tail. Once both yarn tails are through tassel, trim excess yarn.

Hexagon Baby Blanket

Skill Level

EASY

Materials

 in 5 colors (185 yards of each color)

Hook: 5 mm/U.S. H-8
Other: Tapestry needle

Stitches Used

Chain stitch (ch)

Double crochet (dc)

Half double crochet (hdc)

Magic circle

Single crochet (sc)

Slip stitch (sl st)

Instructions

This blanket is made from 35 crocheted hexagons, 7 of each color (here in dark gray, light gray, teal, rose, and ivory).

Hexagon (make 35)

Start with a magic circle.

Round 1: Ch 2, dc in magic circle, ch 2. *2 dc, ch 2; repeat from * 5 times. Sl st to join in top of the first ch 2. (You now have 6 sets of 2 dc + ch 2. The 2 dc are the sides of your hexagon; the ch-2 spaces are the corners.)

Round 2: Ch 3, dc in next dc st. *[In ch-2 sp from previous round: dc, ch 2, dc], dc in next 2 dc; repeat from * 5 more times. Dc, ch 2, dc in last corner sp. Sl st to join in top of first ch 3.

Round 3: Ch 3, dc in next 2 dc. *[In ch-2 sp from previous round: dc, ch 2, dc], dc in next 4 dc; repeat from * 5 more times. Dc, ch 2, dc in last corner sp, dc in next dc. Sl st to join in top of first ch 3.

Round 4: Ch 3, dc in next 3 dc. *[In ch-2 sp from previous round: dc, ch 2, dc], dc in next 6 dc; repeat from * 5 more times. Dc, ch 2, dc in last corner sp, dc in remaining 2 dc. Sl st to join in top of first ch 3.

Round 5: Ch 3, dc in next 4 dc. *[In ch-2 sp from previous round: dc, ch 2, dc], dc in next 8 dc; repeat from * 5 more times. Dc, ch 2, dc in last corner sp, dc in remaining 3 dc. Sl st to join in top of first ch 3.

Fasten off and weave in yarn tails.

Assembly

Arrange your hexagons in a way that looks good to you. This blanket used the following arrangement of alternating rows:

Row 1: Color 1 (here in dark gray), color 2 (here in rose), color 3 (here in ivory), color 4 (here in teal), color 5 (here in light gray)

Row 2: Color 3 (ivory), color 5 (light gray), color 4 (teal), color 2 (rose), color 1 (dark gray)

Continue alternating rows 1 and 2 until all hexagons are used (7 rows total).

See assembly diagram on next page.

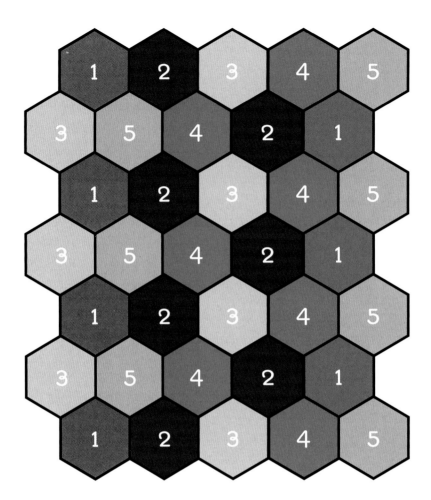

Joining with an Invisible Seam

Once your hexagons are in an arrangement you like, begin joining them using the invisible seam method (also called mattress stitch).

Step 1: Line up 2 hexagons together, right sides facing down. (When you are crocheting a hexagon, the right side is the front side facing you.) Wrong sides should be facing up for joining.

Step 2: Thread tapestry needle with same color yarn as one of the hexagons. Insert needle through back loop of corner chain stitch of first hexagon (here in rose), then through back loop of corresponding corner chain stitch of 2nd hexagon (here in dark gray). Draw yarn through, leaving a tail to weave in later.

insert through back loop only of corner ch sts

Step 3: Insert your tapestry needle through the back loop of the next stitch on the 2nd hexagon (here in dark gray), then through the back loop of the corresponding stitch on the first hexagon (here in rose). Draw yarn through.

Step 4: Insert needle through the back loop of the next stitch on the first hexagon (rose), then through the back loop of the corresponding stitch on the 2nd hexagon (dark gray).

Step 5: Continue working through back loops only of each pair of stitches on the hexagons until end of seam. Once done, you can continue joining other hexagon edges with the same color or fasten off, leaving a tail to weave in later.

Continue joining hexagons using the invisible seam method. Change yarn as needed so the color always matches one of the hexagons you are joining. Once all hexagons are joined together, weave in all remaining yarn tails.

Blanket Border

Attach the border color yarn (here in dark gray) at one hexagon corner.

Border row 1: Ch 2, sc in each st of hexagon sides, including 1 sc in each corner where hexagons are joined. Sl st in top of initial ch 2 to end.

Fasten off and weave in yarn tails.

Hat with Pom-Pom

Skill Level

EASY

Materials

SUPER BULKY

6 1 skein (87 yards)

Hook: 10 mm/U.S. N-15
Other: 2.5" pom-pom maker, scissors, tapestry needle

Stitches Used

Chain stitch (ch)
Half double crochet (hdc)
Half double crochet in back loop only (hdc blo)
Whipstitch

Tip: **Half double crochet in back loop only:**
Yarn over and insert hook under back loop only (rather than under both loops) of next stitch, then complete the hdc as usual: yarn over and draw through first loop on hook, yarn over and draw through all 3 loops on hook to complete the hdc blo.

Instructions

Ch 23.

Row 1: Hdc in 2nd ch from hook. Hdc in each ch st across row.

Row 2: Ch 1, turn. Hdc blo in each st across row until last st. Hdc in last st.

Repeat row 2 until rectangle is the correct size to wrap around head with ridges vertical. This hat has 24 rows. Fasten off, leaving a long tail to sew rectangle together.

Finishing

First, fold short sides of rectangle together. Thread the long yarn tail through a tapestry needle. Join short sides of rectangle together using an invisible seam (see pages 66–67) or a whipstitch (see pages 72–73).

Next, whipstitch along entire top edge of hat tube. (Do not whipstitch two layers of tube together; only work through one layer.) To do this whipstitch edging, insert threaded tapestry needle from front to back under both loops of stitch at edge. Bring needle up over top and insert from front to back through next stitch on left. Pull tight after every couple stitches to bring top of hat together. Repeat across edge of tube, pulling as tight as possible once reaching point where your whipstitches started to close hole completely. Weave in yarn tails.

Finally, make a pom-pom to top hat.

Making a Pom-Pom

Step 1: Open up both arms of the 2.5" pom-pom maker.

Step 2: Wrap yarn around one arm of pom-pom maker about 35 times. The more wraps, the thicker the pom-pom.

Step 3: Bring yarn across the top of center wheel and begin wrapping around other arm of pom-pom maker.

Step 4: Continue wrapping yarn around second arm until you have the same number of wraps as the first arm (35 times in our example).

Step 5: Close both arms of the pom-pom maker. Cut yarn.

Step 6: Place scissors into the groove on one side and cut through center of one wrapped arm. Repeat for other wrapped arm.

Step 7: Cut a length of yarn about 12" long.

Step 8: Wrap yarn around the pom-pom maker, along the groove where you cut.

Step 9: Tie 2 really tight knots on one side.

Step 10: Wrap yarn around to the other side and tie 2 really tight knots on the other side.

Step 11: Open up arms and pull the halves apart to release pom-pom. You will use 2 long yarn tails to sew pom-pom onto hat.

Step 12: Holding pom-pom by 2 long tails, trim ends to shape into a neat ball.

Step 13: Thread one of the long yarn tails through a tapestry needle. Insert needle through top of hat on one side of the closed hole.

Step 14: Draw yarn through to inside of hat. Thread other yarn tail through a tapestry needle.

Step 15: Insert needle through top of hat on other side of closed hole. Draw yarn through on inside.

Step 16: On inside of hat, tie yarn tails in 2 knots. Fasten off and trim excess yarn on inside.

Tip: The completed hat is about 8.5" across and about 11.5" from the top of the pom-pom to the bottom edge of the hat while lying flat.

Chunky Mittens

Skill Level

INTERMEDIATE

Materials

SUPER BULKY 6 2 skeins (212 yards total)

Hooks: 8 mm/U.S. L-11, 9 mm/U.S. M-13
Other: Tapestry needle

Stitches Used

Chain stitch (ch)
Half double crochet (hdc)
Half double crochet in back loop only (hdc blo)
Herringbone half double crochet (Hhdc)
Herringbone half double crochet increase (Hhdc inc)
Herringbone half double crochet 2 together (Hhdc2tog)
Single crochet (sc)
Single crochet 2 together (sc2tog)
Slip stitch (sl st)
Whipstitch

Instructions

Mitten Cuffs (make 2)

With a size 8 mm/U.S. L-11 hook, ch 15.

Row 1: Hdc in 3rd ch from hook. Hdc in each ch st across row. Ch 2, turn.

Rows 2–11: Hdc blo in each st across row. Ch 2, turn.

Row 12: Hdc blo in each st across row. Fasten off, leaving a 12" tail to join cuff with a whipstitch.

Tip: How to hdc blo: Yo, insert hook under back loop only of next stitch, yo, draw through first loop on hook, yo, draw through all 3 loops on hook.

Tip: The finished mittens are about 14" from top of mitten to bottom edge with cuffs unrolled.

Joining with a Whipstitch

Step 1: Thread tapestry needle with 12" yarn tail.

Step 2: Fold short ends of the cuff together so that stitches on both edges are lined up.

Step 3: Insert needle from front to back under the first stitch on each piece.

Step 4: Bring the needle around and insert from front to back under the next pair of stitches.

Step 5: Repeat for each pair of stitches across the seam. Fasten off and weave in yarn tail.

Right and Left Mittens

Using a size 9 mm/U.S. M-13 hook, attach yarn anywhere along one edge of the cuff. Instead of working around in the same direction, you will turn after each round.

Round 1: Ch 2, 12 Hhdc evenly around the cuff, sl st in first Hhdc to join, ch 2, turn.

Round 2: 5 Hhdc, Hhdc inc, Hhdc inc, 5 Hhdc, sl st in first Hhdc to join, ch 2, turn.

Round 3: 6 Hhdc, Hhdc inc, Hhdc inc, 6 Hhdc, sl st in first Hhdc to join, ch 2, turn.

Round 4: 7 Hhdc, Hhdc inc, Hhdc inc, 7 Hhdc, sl st in first Hhdc to join, ch 2, turn.

For rounds 5–14, work one mitten following instructions for right mitten and the other mitten following instructions for left mitten.

Right Mitten

Round 5: 7 Hhdc, ch 2, skip next 5 Hhdc, Hhdc in each of the remaining 6 Hhdc, sl st in first Hhdc to join. Ch 2, turn.

Round 6: Hhdc in each st around (including ch 2 from previous round), sl st in first Hhdc to join. Ch 2, turn.

Rounds 7–12: Hhdc in each st around, sl st in first Hhdc to join. Ch 2, turn.

Round 13: 6 Hhdc, Hhdc2tog, 5 Hhdc, Hhdc2tog, sl st in first Hhdc to join, ch 2, turn.

Round 14: 5 Hhdc, Hhdc2tog, 4 Hhdc, Hhdc2tog, sl st in first Hhdc to join. Fasten off, leaving a 12" tail to close top of mitten.

Left Mitten

Round 5: 6 Hhdc, ch 2, skip next 5 Hhdc, Hhdc in each of the remaining 7 Hhdc, sl st in first Hhdc to join. Ch 2, turn.

Round 6: Hhdc in each st around (including ch 2 from previous round), sl st in first Hhdc to join. Ch 2, turn.

Rounds 7–12: Hhdc in each st around, sl st in first Hhdc to join. Ch 2, turn.

Round 13: 5 Hhdc, Hhdc2tog, 6 Hhdc, Hhdc2tog, sl st in first Hhdc to join. Ch 2, turn.

Round 14: 4 Hhdc, Hhdc2tog, 5 Hhdc, Hhdc2tog, sl st in first Hhdc to join. Fasten off, leaving a 12" tail to close top of mitten.

Tip: **How to sc2tog:** Insert hook in next stitch, yo, draw yarn through stitch, insert hook in next stitch, yo, draw yarn through stitch, yo, draw through all 3 loops on hook to complete.

Tip: **How to Hhdc:** Yo and insert hook into indicated stitch. Yo and pull up a loop by drawing yarn through stitch. You now have 3 loops on hook. Draw that first loop on hook through 2nd loop on hook. You now have 2 loops on hook. Yo and draw through remaining 2 loops on hook to complete the Hhdc.

Tip: **How to Hhdc increase:** Work a Hhdc in next stitch of previous round, inserting hook under top 2 loops of stitch. Work another Hhdc in that same stitch to complete the Hhdc inc.

Tip: **How to Hhdc2tog:** Yo and insert hook under front loop of next stitch, then insert your hook under front loop of next stitch after that without yarning over again (4 loops on hook), yo and draw through first 3 loops on hook (2 loops left on hook), yo and draw through remaining 2 loops on hook to complete the Hhdc2tog.

Closing the Mitten Tops

Thread 12" yarn tail through a tapestry needle. Working in the front loops only of each Hhdc around and from inside the mitten out, stitch loosely around in each stitch. Gently cinch together to close top of mitten. Weave in remaining tail.

Thumb

Using a size 9 mm/U.S. M-13 hook, attach yarn at the right corner of the thumb where rounds 4 and 5 meet. Work counterclockwise.

Round 1: Ch 1, sc2tog, sc, sc2tog, sl st to corner between rounds 4 and 5, 3 sc, sl st to opposite corner between rounds 4 and 5, sl st in top of first sc to join.

Rounds 2–4: Ch 1, sc in each sc around, sl st in top of first sc to join.

Round 5: Ch 1, sc in each sc around, sl st in top of first sc to join. Fasten off, leaving a 12" tail to close top of thumb.

Close top of thumb the same way you closed top of mitten.

Plush Bunny

Skill Level

EASY

Materials

 Velvet yarn, 246 yards

Hook: 5 mm/U.S. H-8

Other: Pins, polyfill stuffing, small pom-pom maker, 2 safety eyes (14 mm/0.55"), 1 safety nose (13 mm/0.51"), stitch marker, tapestry needle

Stitches Used

Chain stitch (ch)

Magic circle

Single crochet (sc)

Single crochet 2 together (sc2tog)

Single crochet increase (sc inc)

Slip stitch (sl st)

Instructions

Place the stitch marker in the first stitch of each round. Move the stitch marker up as you work.

Head

Make a magic circle.

Round 1: 6 sc in magic circle.

Round 2: Sc inc in each st around.

Round 3: *Sc, sc inc; repeat from * around.

Round 4: *2 sc, sc inc; repeat from * around.

Round 5: *3 sc, sc inc; repeat from * around.

Round 6: *4 sc, sc inc; repeat from * around.

Round 7: *5 sc, sc inc; repeat from * around.

Round 8: *6 sc, sc inc; repeat from * around.

Round 9: *7 sc, sc inc; repeat from * around.

Rounds 10–20: Sc in each st around.

Tip: **How to sc increase:** Work a single crochet into next stitch. Work another single crochet into that same stitch to complete the sc inc.

Adding the Eyes and Nose

Step 1: From the front (right) side of the bunny's head, push one of the safety eyes through a space between stitches in rounds 15 and 16 from front to back.

Step 2: Attach the plastic washer to the safety eye from the back (wrong) side, inside the bunny's head.

Step 3: From the front (right) side of the bunny's head, add other safety eye approximately 8 stitches over from the first eye between rounds 15 and 16 as shown below. From the back (wrong) side, inside the bunny's head, attach washer to 2nd safety eye.

Step 4: From the front (right) side of the bunny's head, insert the safety nose 2 rounds down and centered between the eyes.

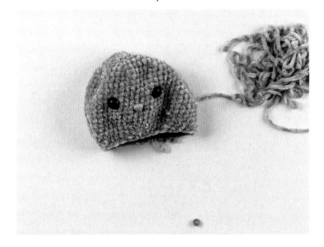

Step 5: From the back (wrong) side, inside the bunny's head, attach the plastic washer to the nose.

After adding safety eyes and nose, begin stuffing head with polyfill as you continue each round.

Round 21: *7 sc, sc2tog; repeat from * around.

Round 22: *6 sc, sc2tog; repeat from * around.

Round 23: *5 sc, sc2tog; repeat from * around.

Round 24: *4 sc, sc2tog; repeat from * around.

Round 25: *3 sc, sc2tog; repeat from * around.

Round 26: *2 sc, sc2tog; repeat from * around.

Round 27: *Sc, sc2tog; repeat from * around.

Round 28: Sc2tog around.

Finish stuffing head with polyfill.

Fasten off, leaving a long tail with which to close the remaining hole and sew the head onto the body later.

Tip: **How to sc2tog:** [Insert hook in next stitch, yo, draw yarn through stitch] 2 times, yo, draw yarn through all 3 loops on hook to complete the sc2tog.

Body

The body will begin at the bottom of the legs and work up to the top. Stuff with polyfill as you go.

Make a magic circle.

Round 1: 6 sc in magic circle.

Round 2: Sc inc in each st around.

Round 3: *Sc, sc inc; repeat from * around.

Rounds 4–28: Sc in each st around.

Fasten off. Repeat above for 2nd leg, but do not fasten off after round 28.

Ch 3.

Round 29: Sc into the next stitch of the first leg, and in each stitch around and over the 3 chains to the second leg until you reach your stitch marker.

Rounds 30–45: Sc in each st around.

Round 46: *4 sc, sc2tog; repeat from * around.

Round 47: *3 sc, sc2tog; repeat from * around.

Round 48: *2 sc, sc2tog; repeat from * around.

Round 49: *Sc, sc2tog; repeat from * around.

Round 50: Sc in each st around.

Fasten off.

Arms (make 2)

Stuff arms with polyfill as you go.

Make a magic circle.

Round 1: 6 sc in magic circle.

Rounds 2–22: Sc in each st around.

Fasten off, leaving a long tail with which to sew arms onto body.

Ears (make 2)

Do not stuff ears.

Make a magic circle.

Round 1: 6 sc in magic circle.

Round 2: Sc inc in each st around.

Round 3: *Sc, sc inc; repeat from * around.

Rounds 4–16: Sc in each st around.

Round 17: Sc2tog in each st around.

Fasten off, leaving a long tail with which to sew ears onto head.

Tail

Using the 4/medium yarn of your choice and a small pom-pom maker, make a pom-pom tail, following the instructions on pages 69–71 as a guide. We used less than 3 yards of a contrasting white yarn, but you can also use the same velvet yarn as the rest of the bunny. You will have enough leftover velvet yarn from which to make the pom-pom tail. Leave 2 long ends to attach tail to body.

Assembly

Thread the long tail left from the head through a tapestry needle. Sew head securely to body all the way around. Pin arms to body in desired position. Thread long tail from arm through tapestry needle. Sew arms onto body. Pin ears to head in desired position. Thread long tail from ear through tapestry needle. Sew ears onto head. Attach pom-pom tail to back of body using 2 long ends. Weave in all yarn tails when done.

Tip: This completed bunny is about 15" tall from top of head to bottom of legs.

Tip: Stitch markers

Stitch markers are especially critical when crocheting amigurumi. Because you frequently do not join at the end of each round, you need to know exactly which stitch marks the beginning and/or end of each round.

Infinity Scarf

Skill Level

BEGINNER

Materials

BULKY 5 1 skein (312 yards)

Hook: 6 mm/U.S. J-10
Other: Tapestry needle

Stitches Used

Chain stitch (ch)
Double crochet (dc)
Slip stitch (sl st)
V-stitch

Tip: **How to make the v-stitch:** [dc, ch 1, dc] in one stitch or space.

Instructions

Ch 25.

Row 1: Dc in 4th ch from hook, dc in same st, *skip 2 sts, v-stitch in next st; repeat from * across row. Ch 1, turn.

Row 2: V-stitch in the ch-1 sp from the v-stitch in previous row, *skip 2 spaces, v-stitch in next ch-1 sp; repeat from * across row. Ch 1, turn.

Rows 3–80 (or desired length): Repeat row 2.

Finishing

Once reaching desired length, fold scarf in half with the 2 short ends together. Join the short ends with a slip stitch through both layers. Fasten off and weave in yarn tails.

slip stitch seam

Tip: The finished scarf is about 22.5" long and 7" wide when joined.

Ridged Baby Bib

Skill Level

▉ ▉ ▢ ▢
EASY

Materials

 Cotton yarn, less than 200 yards

Hook: 5 mm/U.S. H-8
Other: Tapestry needle, 2 half-inch buttons

Stitches Used

Chain stitch (ch)
Single crochet (sc)
Single crochet in back loop only (sc blo)
Single crochet 2 together in back loops only (sc2tog blo)
Slip stitch (sl st)

Instructions

Ch 57.

Row 1: Sc in 2nd ch from hook and in each ch st across row.

Row 2: Ch 1, turn. *Sc blo in next 13 sc, 2 sc blo in next sc; rep from * to end of row.

Row 3: Ch 2, turn. *Sc blo in next 14 sc, 2 sc in next sc; rep from * to end of row.

Row 4 (buttonhole row): Ch 1, turn. Sc blo in next 2 sc, ch 1, sk next sc (first buttonhole), sc blo in next 6 sc, ch 1, sk next sc (2nd buttonhole), sc blo in next 5 sc, 2 sc blo in next sc. *Sc blo in next 15 sc, 2 sc blo in next sc; rep from * to end of row.

Row 5: Ch 1, turn. *Sc blo in next 16 sc, 2 sc blo in next sc; rep from * to end of row.

Row 6: Ch 1, turn. *Sc blo in next 17 sc, 2 sc blo in next sc; rep from * to end of row.

Row 7: Ch 1, turn. *Sc blo in next 18 sc, 2 sc blo in next sc; rep from * to end of row.

Row 8: Ch 1, turn. Sl st in next 20 sc, sc blo in next sc, sc2tog blo, sc blo in next 16 sc, [2 sc blo in next sc] twice, sc blo in next 16 sc, sc2tog blo, sc blo in next sc. Remaining sc in row will stay unworked.

Row 9: Ch 1, turn. Sc blo in first sc, sc2tog blo, sc blo in next 16 sc, [2 sc blo in next sc] twice, sc blo in next 16 sc, sc2tog blo, sc blo in last sc.

Rows 10–126: Repeat row 9. Fasten off and weave in yarn tails.

⌒ip: **How to sc blo:** Insert hook under back loop only (rather than under both top loops) of next stitch, then complete the sc as usual: yo and draw yarn through first loop on hook, yo and draw yarn through both loops on hook to complete the sc blo.

⌒ip: **How to sc2tog blo:** Insert hook under back loop only of next stitch, yo and draw through stitch (2 loops on hook), insert hook under back loop only of next stitch (3 loops on hook), yo and draw through all 3 loops on hook to complete the sc2tog blo.

Sewing on the Buttons

Sew buttons in place on strap opposite buttonhole strap. Position straps so buttonholes overlap strap where you'll sew on buttons. Mark where buttons will go with pins or stitch markers, if desired. Place first button in center of collar strap, and second button about 1¾" up from first button (or whatever correct distance is for your bib).

Step 1: Thread tapestry needle with matching yarn. If holes in buttons are too narrow for a tapestry needle, use a sewing needle and thread.

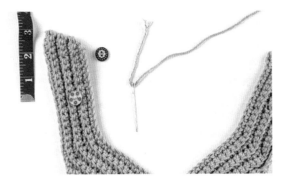

Step 2: Insert needle from the back (wrong) side of the bib up through 1 button hole to the front (right) side, leaving a tail on the back side.

Step 3: Insert needle from front to back through the other button hole. Pull tight.

Step 4: Insert needle from back to front through the first button hole again. Insert needle from front to back through other button hole. Repeat until you feel button is secure.

Step 5: On the back (wrong) side, trim yarn. Tie a knot with the yarn tails.

Step 6: Tie a second tight knot to secure. Trim or weave in yarn tails.

Crochet Fox

Skill Level

INTERMEDIATE

Materials

 in orange, black, and white (much less than 1 skein of each)

Hook: 3.5 mm/U.S. E-4
Other: Pins, polyfill stuffing, 2 safety eyes (13 mm/0.51"), 1 safety nose (13 mm/0.51" wide, 9 mm/0.35" tall), stitch marker, tapestry needle

Stitches Used

Chain stitch (ch)

Magic circle

Single crochet (sc)

Single crochet 2 together (sc2tog)

Single crochet 3 together (sc3tog)

Single crochet increase (sc inc)

3 single crochet increase (3-sc inc)

Whipstitch

Instructions

Place the stitch marker in the first stitch of each round. Move the stitch marker up as you work.

Body

Using orange yarn, make a magic circle.

Round 1: 4 sc inside the magic circle.

Round 2: 3-sc inc in each sc around.

Round 3: Sc in next st, 3-sc inc in next st. *2 sc, 3-sc inc; rep from * 3 times and sc in next st.

Round 4: 2 sc, 3-sc inc. *4 sc, 3-sc inc; rep from * 3 times and sc in next 2 sts.

Round 5: 3 sc, 3-sc inc. *6 sc, 3-sc inc; rep from * 3 times and sc in next 3 sts.

Round 6: 4 sc, 3-sc inc. *8 sc, 3-sc inc; rep from * 3 times and sc in next 4 sts.

Round 7: 5 sc, sc2tog. *9 sc, sc2tog; rep from * 3 times and sc in next 4 sts.

Tip: How to 3-sc inc:

Work a single crochet in stitch of previous round. Work a 2nd single crochet in that same stitch. Work a 3rd single crochet in that same stitch to complete the 3-sc increase.

Tip: How to sc2tog:

[Insert hook in next stitch, yarn over, draw yarn through stitch] 2 times, yarn over, draw yarn through all 3 loops on hook to complete the sc2tog.

Tip: How to sc3tog:

[Insert hook in next stitch, yarn over, draw yarn through stitch] 3 times, yarn over, draw yarn through all 4 loops on hook to complete the sc3tog.

Rounds 8–13: 40 sc around.

Round 14: 4 sc, sc3tog. *7 sc, sc3tog; rep from * 3 times and sc in next 3 sts.

Round 15: 3 sc, sc3tog. *5 sc, sc3tog; rep from * 3 times and sc in next 2 sts.

Place safety eyes between rounds 11 and 12, approximately 6 stitches apart (see page 77 for adding safety eyes). Stuff generously with polyfill. It takes more stuffing than you might think!

Round 16: 2 sc, sc3tog. *3 sc, sc3tog; rep from * 3 times, sc in next st.

Round 17: *Sc, sc3tog; rep from * 4 times.

Closing the Body

Step 1: After adding more stuffing, thread yarn tail through a tapestry needle.

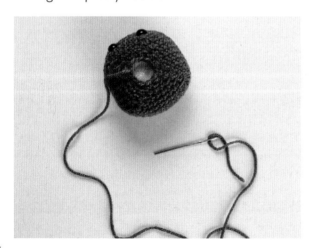

Step 2: Insert threaded needle under the back loop only.

Step 3: Continue to insert needle under back loops only, working your way around, pulling every 3 stitches or so to start closing the hole.

Step 4: Once hole is completely closed, fasten off and weave in the tail.

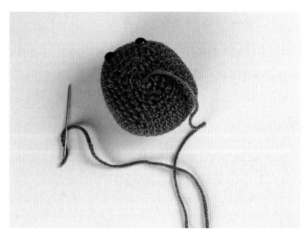

Snout

Using white yarn, make a magic circle.

Round 1: 5 sc in the magic circle.

Round 2: *Sc, sc3tog; rep from * 4 times.

Round 3: *Sc, sc inc; rep from * 4 times. Fasten off, leaving a long tail for sewing. Add safety nose to center of snout.

Tip: **How to sc increase:** Work a single crochet in next stitch of previous round, inserting hook under top 2 loops of stitch. Work another single crochet in that same stitch to complete the sc inc.

Ears (make 2)

Starting with black yarn, make a magic circle.

Round 1: 5 sc in the magic circle.

Round 2: Switch to orange yarn. Sc inc, sc, sc inc, sc, sc inc.

Round 3: *4 sc, sc inc; rep from * 4 times.

Round 4: *3 sc, sc inc; rep from * 3 times.

Round 5: *4 sc, sc inc; rep from * 3 times.

Round 6: 18 sc. Fasten off, leaving a long tail for sewing.

Pinch open side of ear closed so it lies flat. Sew shut with a whipstitch (**see pages 72–73**).

Tail

Starting with white yarn, make a magic circle.

Round 1: 5 sc in the magic circle.

Round 2: Sc inc in each st around.

Round 3: Sc in each st around.

Round 4: *Sc inc, 2 sc; rep from * 2 times.

Round 5: Switch to orange yarn. *Sc inc, 2 sc; rep from * 4 times.

Round 6: *Sc inc, 3 sc; rep from * 4 times.

Rounds 7–8: Sc in each st around.

Round 9: *Sc2tog, 3 sc; rep from * 4 times.

Round 10: Sc in each st around.

Round 11: *Sc2tog, 2 sc; rep from * 4 times.

Rounds 12–13: Sc in each st around.

Round 14: *Sc2tog, 2 sc; rep from * 3 times.

Round 15: Sc in each st around.

Round 16: *Sc2tog, sc; rep from * 2 times. Fasten off, leaving a long tail for sewing. Stuff lightly with polyfill, if desired.

Legs (make 4)

Starting with black yarn, make a magic circle.

Round 1: 5 sc in the magic circle.

Round 2: Sc inc in each st around.

Round 3: Sc in each st around.

Rounds 4–7: Switch to orange yarn. Sc in each st around. Fasten off, leaving a long tail for sewing.

Assembly

Step 1: Position snout on fox body, centered between safety eyes, approximately over rounds 10–13. Thread white yarn tail from snout through a tapestry needle.

Step 2: Sew onto body, going through white stitches only, around entire snout.

Step 3: When snout is secured on body, bring the needle out several stitches away through the orange part of the body, as shown below. Trim excess yarn.

Step 4: Pin 4 unstuffed legs in a position you like under fox body. You want the legs to lie flat against the bottom of the body.

Step 5: Thread orange yarn tail from leg through tapestry needle. Sew leg onto bottom of body. Repeat for other legs.

Step 6: Sew the tail on the back of the body, approximately over rounds 11–12, using yarn tail left from the tail and a tapestry needle.

Step 7: Pin 2 unstuffed ears in a position you like on top of head. Using orange yarn tail from ears and a tapestry needle, sew ears onto body at top of head.

Step 8: Weave in all yarn tails when done.

Lacy Scarf

Skill Level

EASY

Materials

SUPER FINE

1 3 skeins (approx. 498 yards total)

Hook: 3.5 mm/U.S. E-4

Other: Blocking boards, rustproof T pins, spray bottle of water, tapestry needle

Stitches Used

Chain stitch (ch)

Double crochet (dc)

Single crochet (sc)

Shell stitch

Tip: **How to make the shell stitch:** Make 5 dc in 1 stitch. The top of each shell is the 3rd dc of the 5-dc shell.

Instructions

Ch 44.

Row 1: Sc in 8th ch from hook. *Ch 5, sk 3 ch, sc; rep from * across row.

Row 2: Ch 6, turn. Sc in ch-5 sp, 5-dc shell in next sc, sc in ch-5 sp. *Ch 5, sc in ch-5 sp, 5-dc shell in next sc, sc in ch-5 sp; rep from * across to last ch-sp and ch 5, sc in last sp.

Row 3: Ch 6, turn. Sc in top of 5-dc shell (3rd or center dc of the shell). *Ch 5, sc in ch-5 sp, ch 5, sc in top of 5-dc shell; rep from * across to last ch-sp and ch 5, sc in last sp.

Row 4: Ch 3, turn. 3 dc in sc, sc in ch-5 sp, ch 5, sc in ch-5 sp. *5-dc shell in next sc, sc in ch-5 sp, ch 5, sc in ch-5 sp; rep from * across to last ch-sp, sc in last sp.

Row 5: Ch 6, turn. Sc in ch-5 sp. *Ch 5, sc in top of 5-dc shell, ch 5, sc in ch-5 sp; rep from * across row, ending with a ch 5, sc in top of ch 3 from row 4.

Repeat rows 2–5 until desired length. Fasten off and weave in yarn tails.

Blocking the Scarf

Blocking goes a long way toward giving your crocheted project a finished, professional look. Blocking helps edges lie flat, makes pieces easier to join, and forces your crocheted project to dry in the proper shape. Blocking this scarf will make stitches look less crumpled and more consistent. It will also make the scarf longer and wider. This completed scarf is about 54" long and 10" wide after blocking.

Step 1: Prepare a blocking board long enough for your scarf. You can purchase foam blocking boards like these, which fit together, or use another flat, padded surface such as a piece of Styrofoam or corkboard, an ironing board, or a towel-covered couch.

Step 2: Mist scarf with a spray bottle of water until evenly saturated.

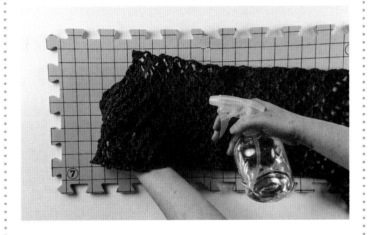

Step 3: Stretch damp scarf into desired shape on foam blocking boards (or other prepared surface) and pin around edges using lots of rustproof T pins. Leave undisturbed until completely dry.

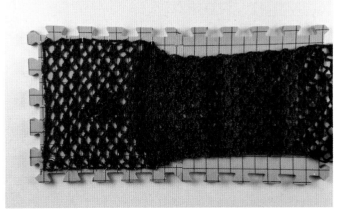

Removable Pillow Cover

Skill Level

EASY

Materials

 SUPER BULKY 2 skeins (87 yards each)

Hook: 6 mm/U.S. J-10

Other: 12" x 12" pillow form, 12" zipper, pins, sewing needle, tapestry needle, thread

Stitches Used

Chain stitch (ch)
Half double crochet (hdc)
Slip stitch (sl st)
Whipstitch

Instructions

This removable pillow cover is worked in rounds, creating a large tube.

Ch 72. Join with a sl st to the first chain you made to form a ring.

Round 1: Ch 2, sl st in next ch. *Hdc in next ch, sl st in next ch; repeat from * around. Join with a sl st in top of beginning ch 2. Ch 2, turn.

Round 2: Sl st in next hdc. *Hdc in next ch, sl st in next ch; repeat from * around. Join with a sl st in top of beginning ch 2. Ch 2, turn.

Repeat round 2 until size of cover matches size of pillow. This pillow cover is 32 rounds.

Fasten off and weave in yarn tails.

Finishing

Whipstitch one open end of the tube closed using yarn and a tapestry needle. (See pages 72–73 for whipstitch instructions.)

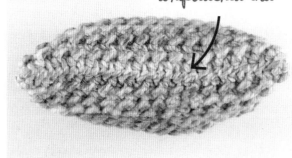

whipstitched end

Tip: How to whipstitch

Hold sides of pillow cover tube with right sides (outward-facing) together and stitches lined up. Insert threaded yarn needle from front to back under the first pair of stitches on the right. Draw yarn through, leaving a tail to weave in later. Bring needle back around and insert from front to back under the next pair of stitches on the left. Repeat for each pair of stitches across the seam. Fasten off and weave in yarn tails.

Sew a zipper into the other open end of the tube.

Sewing in the Zipper

Step 1: Pin one side of the closed zipper, right side facing out, to one inside (wrong side) edge of the pillow cover.

Step 2: Thread a sewing needle with a long piece of matching thread and knot one end. Beginning on the inside (wrong side) at one end, sew zipper onto pillow cover using a running stitch.

Step 3: Continue sewing a running stitch across to end of zipper. Tie a knot and trim excess thread.

Step 4: Pin other side of closed zipper to opposite edge of pillow cover as shown. Open zipper once it's pinned in place and sew onto inside edge of pillow cover with a running stitch as you did for first side.

Step 5: After the zipper is sewn in, add the 12" x 12" pillow form to complete the project.

Mandala Wall Hanging

Skill Level

EASY

Materials

 in 3 colors

Hook: 5 mm/U.S. H-8

Other: 8" embroidery hoop, tapestry needle

Stitches Used

Chain stitch (ch)

Double crochet (dc)

Double crochet increase (dc inc)

Magic circle

Single crochet (sc)

Single crochet increase (sc inc)

Slip stitch (sl st)

Tip: This project doesn't take much yarn and is a great way to use up yarn scraps! This example uses 3 colors: color 1 is white, color 2 is orange, and color 3 is blue.

Instructions

With color 1 (white), make a magic circle.

Round 1: Ch 3, make 11 dc into the magic circle. Sl st in top of ch 3 to complete round.

Change to color 2 (orange).

Round 2: Ch 3, dc inc in each st around. Sl st in top of ch 3 to complete round.

Change to color 3 (blue).

Round 3: Ch 1, *sc, sc inc; repeat from * around. Sl st in top of ch 1 to complete round.

Change to color 2 (orange).

Round 4: Ch 1, *2 sc, sc inc; repeat from * around. Sl st in top of ch 1 to complete round.

Change to color 1 (white).

Round 5: Ch 3, *3 dc, dc inc; repeat from * around. Sl st in top of ch 3 to complete round.

Change to color 3 (blue).

Round 6: Ch 1, *4 sc, sc inc; repeat from * around. Sl st in top of ch 3 to complete round.

Round 7: Ch 3, dc in each st around. Sl st in top of ch 3 to complete round.

Tip: How to sc increase: Work a single crochet into next stitch of previous round, inserting your hook under the top 2 loops of stitch. Work a 2nd single crochet into that same stitch to complete the sc increase.

Tip: How to dc increase: Work a double crochet into the next stitch of previous round, inserting your hook under the top 2 loops of stitch. Work a 2nd double crochet into that same stitch to complete the dc increase.

Attaching the Hoop

Place mandala inside inner embroidery hoop (see picture 1). Unscrew and remove outer embroidery hoop. Set aside for now.

Attach mandala to inner embroidery hoop with a single crochet in each stitch around: Insert hook through hoop and into next stitch (as seen in picture 2). *Working under hoop*: yarn over and draw through first loop on hook. You will have 2 loops on hook. *Working above hoop* (as seen in picture 3): yarn over and draw through both loops on hook. You will have 1 loop on hook each time you complete a single crochet (as seen in picture 4).

The first few stitches around the hoop can be tricky but it will become easier as you go. Continue to single crochet in each stitch around, doing your first yarn over and draw through under the hoop, then completing the single crochet over the hoop with the 2nd yarn over. Fasten off and weave in yarn tail. Replace outer embroidery hoop and tighten screw.

Picture 1

working above hoop

Picture 3

work first part of stitch under hoop

Picture 2

Picture 4

Chunky Throw Blanket

Instructions

With color 1 (here in green), ch 81.

Row 1: 2 dc in 3rd ch from hook, *sk 2 ch sts, [sc, 2 dc] in next ch; rep from * across until last 3 ch sts. Sk 2 ch sts, sc in last ch st. Ch 1, turn.

Row 2: 2 dc in next st, *sk 2 sts, [sc, 2 dc] in next st; rep from * across until the last 3 sts, sk 2 sts, sc in top of turning ch. Ch 1, turn.

Repeat row 2 until desired size, alternating between color 1 (green) and color 2 (gray) however often you like. In this example, 3 skeins (108 yards each) of color 1 (green) were used before switching to color 2 (gray). All 431 yards of color 2 (gray) were used before switching back to color 1 (green). Then 3 more skeins of color 1 (green) were used to finish the blanket. Fasten off and weave in all yarn tails when done.

Skill Level

BEGINNER

Materials

SUPER BULKY 6

648 yards of color 1 (green), 431 yards of color 2 (gray)

Hook: 15 mm / U.S. P
Other: Tapestry needle

Stitches Used

Chain stitch (ch)
Double crochet (dc)
Single crochet (sc)

Tip: This finished blanket is only about 43" by 37". For a larger blanket, add more chains to the foundation and more repeats of row 2.

Ear Warmer

Skill Level

EASY

Materials

SUPER BULKY **6** 50 yards

Hook: 10 mm/U.S. N-15
Other: Tapestry needle

Stitches Used

Chain stitch (ch)
Double crochet (dc)
Single crochet (sc)
Single crochet 2 together (sc2tog)
Slip stitch (sl st)
Whipstich

Instructions

Ch 35.

Row 1: 5 sc, *sk 1 st, [sc, dc] in next st; rep from * until last 4 sts of row, sc in last 4 sts. Ch 1, turn.

Row 2: 4 sc, *sk next st, [sc, dc] in next st; rep from * leaving last 5 sts unworked. Ch 1, turn.

Row 3: *Sk next st, [sc, dc] in next st; rep from * leaving last 4 sts unworked. Ch 1, turn.

Row 4: *Sk next st, [sc, dc] in next st; rep from * until last 5 sts of row, sc2tog beginning in last dc worked and ending in first unworked st from row 2. Sc in remaining 4 sts. Ch 1, turn.

Row 5: 5 sc, *sk next st, [sc, dc] in next st; rep from * until last 4 sts of row, sc2tog beginning in last dc worked and ending in first unworked st from row 3. Sc in remaining 3 sts. Ch 1, turn.

Row 6: 4 sc, *sk next st, [sc, dc] in next st; rep from * until last 5 sts, sc in last 5 sts. Fasten off, leaving a long tail for joining.

Finishing

Thread yarn tail through tapestry needle. Fold ear warmer in half with short ends together. Whipstitch (see pages 72–73) through both short ends to create a circle. Weave in yarn tails when done.

Tip: This ear warmer is about 11" long and 5" wide when joined with a whipstitch.

Pet Bed

Hook: 10 mm/U.S. N-15
Other: Tapestry needle

Skill Level

BEGINNER

Materials

 3 skeins (less than 600 yards total)

Stitches Used

Chain stitch (ch)
Double crochet (dc)
Double crochet increase (dc inc)
Magic circle
Single crochet (sc)
Slip stitch (sl st)

Instructions

Work entire pattern using 3 strands of yarn held together at the same time, treating the 3 strands as 1 strand.

Make a magic circle.

Round 1: Ch 3, 11 dc into magic circle. Join with a sl st to top of first ch 3.

Round 2: Ch 2, dc inc in each st around. Join with a sl st to top of first dc.

Round 3: Ch 2, *dc inc, dc; rep from * around. Join with a sl st to top of first dc.

Round 4: Ch 2, *dc inc, 2 dc; rep from * around. Join with a sl st to top of first dc.

Round 5: Ch 2, *dc inc, 3 dc; rep from * around. Join with a sl st to top of first dc.

Round 6: Ch 2, *dc inc, 4 dc; rep from * around. Join with a sl st to top of first dc.

Round 7: Ch 2, *dc inc, 5 dc; rep from * around. Join with a sl st to top of first dc.

Rounds 8–10: Ch 2, dc in each st around. Join with a sl st to top of first dc.

Round 11: Ch 1, sc in each st around. Join with a sl st to top of first sc. Fasten off and weave in yarn tails.

Tip: The finished pet bed is about 16" across, so works best for a small pet.

Tip: **Double crochet increase**
Work a double crochet into next stitch of previous round. Work a 2nd double crochet into that same stitch to complete the dc inc.

Tip: **Multi-strand crochet**
Crocheting with multiple strands of yarn at the same time will result in a thicker, sturdier finished project. You can also create your own unique color blends with multi-strand crochet. For this project, the 3 strands of yarn are coming from 3 different colored skeins. Hold the 3 strands together the entire time, effectively treating them as 1 strand of yarn. Pull the yarn from the center of each skein. To prevent tangling, try using yarn bowls like the one shown below.

Granny Bag

Skill Level

EASY

Materials

 in 2 colors (372 yards of each)

Hook: 4 mm/U.S. G-6
Other: 4 stitch markers, tapestry needle

Stitches Used

Chain stitch (ch)
Double crochet (dc)
Magic circle
Single crochet (sc)
Slip stitch (sl st)

Instructions

Using color 1 (here in tan), make a magic circle.

Round 1: Working into magic circle: ch 3, 3 dc, *(ch 2, 4 dc); rep from * 3 times. Sl st to top of first ch 3 to close round.

Round 2: Ch 3, (dc, ch 2, 2 dc) into ch-2 sp, dc in each st around, working (2 dc, ch 2, 2 dc) in each ch-2 sp. Sl st in top of first ch 3 to close round.

Round 3: Ch 3, dc in each st around, working (2 dc, ch 2, 2 dc) in each ch-2 sp. Sl st in top of first ch 3 to close round.

Rounds 4–11: Repeat round 3. At the end of round 11, fasten off and weave in yarn tails.

Counting in from 2 corner ch-2 spaces, place a stitch marker in the center 2 stitches of that round and repeat for all 4 sides (you will need 4 stitch markers).

Using color 1 (tan) again, attach in any corner ch-2 sp to begin round 12.

Round 12: Ch 3, (dc, ch 2, 2 dc) into ch-2 sp, *dc in each st until 1 st before the marker, skip 4 sts, dc in each st until next ch-2 sp, (2 dc, ch 2, 2 dc) in each ch-2 sp; rep from * around. Sl st in top of first ch 3 to close round.

Round 13: Ch 3, dc in each st around, skipping the 4 middle sts of each side and working (2 dc, ch 2, 2 dc) in each ch-2 sp. Sl st in top of first ch 3 to close round. Fasten off and weave in tails.

Change to color 2 (here in navy blue) and attach in any corner ch-2 sp to begin round 14.

Round 14: Ch 3, (dc, ch 2, 2 dc) into ch-2 sp, dc in each st around, skipping the middle 4 sts of each side and working (2 dc, ch 2, 2 dc) in each ch-2 sp. Sl st in top of first ch 3 to close round.

Rounds 15–21: Ch 3, dc in each st around, skipping the middle 4 sts of each side and working (2 dc, ch 2, 2 dc) in each ch-2 sp. Sl st in top of first ch 3 to close round. Fasten off and weave in tails after the end of round 21.

skipped 4 middle stitches

Change to color 1 (tan) and attach in any corner ch-2 sp to begin round 22.

Round 22: Ch 3, (dc, ch 2, 2 dc) into ch-2 sp, dc in each st around, skipping the middle 4 sts of each side and working (2 dc, ch 2, 2 dc) in each ch-2 sp. Sl st in top of first ch 3 to close round.

Round 23: Ch 3, dc in each st around, skipping the middle 4 sts of each side and working (2 dc, ch 2, 2 dc) in each ch-2 sp. Sl st in top of first ch 3 to close round. Fasten off and weave in tails.

Change to color 2 (navy blue) and attach in any corner ch-2 sp to begin round 24.

Round 24: Ch 3, (dc, ch 2, 2 dc) into ch-2 sp, dc in each st around, skipping the middle 4 sts of each side and working (2 dc, ch 2, 2 dc) in each ch-2 sp. Sl st in top of first ch 3 to close round.

Rounds 25–27: Ch 3, dc in each st around, skipping the middle 4 sts of each side and working (2 dc, ch 2, 2 dc) in each ch-2 sp. Sl st in top of first ch 3 to close round. Fasten off and weave in tails after the end of round 27.

Round 28: Ch 3, (dc, ch 2, 2 dc) into ch-2 sp, dc in each st around, skipping middle 4 sts of each side and working (2 dc, ch 2, 2 dc) in each ch-2 sp. Sl st in top of first ch 3 to close round. Fasten off and weave in tails.

Straps

Using color 1 (tan), attach in any corner ch-2 sp and ch 60. Join with a sl st to the next corner ch-2 sp and fasten off.

Repeat above for 2nd strap, using remaining 2 corner ch-2 sp. Do not fasten off after joining with a sl st to the corner ch-2 sp.

Round 1: Ch 1, sc in each st around and into each ch of the straps. Sl st into the first sc to join and end round. Fasten off and weave in tails.

Tip: The finished bag is about 13" wide and just under 18" tall from the base to a top peak. Each strap is about 17" long.

Potholder

Skill Level

BEGINNER

Materials

 MEDIUM 4 less than 120 yards

Hook: 6.5 mm/U.S. K-10.5
Other: Tapestry needle

Stitches Used

Chain stitch (ch)
Half double crochet (hdc)
Slip stitch (sl st)

Tip: The finished potholder is about 8" by 8".

Instructions

Work pattern using 2 strands of yarn held together at the same time, treating the 2 strands as 1 strand. This will create a thicker potholder. Both strands of yarn are coming from the same skein for this project. Pull 1 strand from the center of the skein and 1 strand from the outside of the skein.

Ch 20.

Row 1: Sl st in 2nd ch from hook. *Hdc, sl st; repeat from * across row. Ch 1, turn.

Rows 2–22: Sl st in first st, *hdc, sl st; repeat from * across row. Ch 1, turn.

Ch 10. Sl st into base of ch 10 to create a loop.

Fasten off and weave in yarn tails.

Tip: Because this pattern is worked with 2 strands of yarn held together, each yarn over and resulting loop on your hook will consist of 2 strands. Treat each set of 2 loops on your hook as 1 loop regardless of which stitch you are performing.

Striped Baby Blanket

Skill Level

EASY

Materials

 in 4 colors (370 yards of each)

Hook: 5 mm/U.S. H-8
Other: Tapestry needle

Stitches Used

Chain stitch (ch)
Back post double crochet (BPdc)
Double crochet (dc)
Front post double crochet (FPdc)
Half double crochet (hdc)
Herringbone half double crochet (Hhdc)
Single crochet (sc)

Tip: **How to FPdc:** Yo and insert hook under post of next stitch from the front side. Yo and draw yarn around post. Yo and draw yarn through first 2 loops on hook. Yo and draw yarn through remaining 2 loops on hook to complete the FPdc.

Tip: **How to BPdc:** Yo and insert hook under post of next stitch from the back side. Yo and draw yarn around post. Yo and draw yarn through first 2 loops on hook. Yo and draw through remaining 2 loops on hook to complete the BPdc.

Tip: **How to Hhdc:** Yo and insert hook into next stitch. Yo, draw yarn through stitch and next loop on hook. You now have 2 loops on hook. Yo and draw yarn through remaining 2 loops on hook to complete the Hhdc.

Instructions

Using color 1 (here in white), ch 120.

Row 1: Dc in 4th ch from hook, dc in each ch across row. Ch 2, turn.

Row 2: Dc in same st as ch 2, *FPdc around next st, dc in next st; rep from * across row, ending with a dc in last st. Ch 2, turn.

Row 3: Dc in same st as ch 2, *BPdc around FPdc from previous row, dc in next st; rep from * across row, ending with a dc in last st. Change to color 2 (here in aqua) and fasten off previous color. Ch 1, turn.

Row 4: Sc in each st across row. Ch 1, turn.

FPdc & BPdc rows

Hhdc rows

Rows 5–20: Hhdc in each st across row. Ch 1, turn.

Row 21: Sc in each st across row. Change to color 1 (white) and fasten off previous color. Ch 1, turn.

Row 22: Sc in each st across row. Ch 1, turn.

Row 23: Sc in each st across row. Change to color 3 (here in light gray-blue) and fasten off previous color. Ch 1, turn.

Rows 24–41: Hdc in first st, *sk next st, [sc, hdc] in next st; rep from * across until last st, sc in last st. Ch 1, turn.

Row 42: Sc in each st across row. Change to color 1 (white) and fasten off previous color. Ch 1, turn.

Row 43: Sc in each st across row. Ch 1, turn.

Row 44: Sc in each st across row. Change to color 4 (here in dark blue) and fasten off previous color. Ch 1, turn.

Row 45: Sc in each st across row. Ch 1, turn.

Rows 46–61: Hhdc in each st across row. Ch 1, turn.

Row 62: Sc in each st across row. Change to color 1 (white) and fasten off previous color. Ch 1, turn.

Rows 63–64: Sc in each st across row. Ch 1, turn. After row 64, change to color 2 (aqua) and fasten off previous color.

Row 65: Sc in each st across row. Ch 1, turn.

Rows 66–83: Hdc in first st, *sk next st, [sc, hdc] in next st; rep from * across until last st, sc in last st. Ch 1, turn.

Row 84: Sc in each st across row. Change to color 1 (white) and fasten off previous color.

Ch 1, turn.

Rows 85–86: Sc in each st across row. Ch 1, turn. After row 86, change to color 3 (light gray-blue) and fasten off previous color.

Row 87: Sc in each st across row. Ch 1, turn.

Rows 88–103: Hhdc in each st across row. Ch 1, turn.

Row 104: Sc in each st across row. Change to color 1 (white) and fasten off previous color. Ch 1, turn.

Rows 105–106: Sc in each st across row. Ch 1, turn. After row 106, change to color 4 (dark blue) and fasten off previous color.

Row 107: Sc in each st across row. Ch 1, turn.

Rows 108–125: Hdc in first st, *sk next st, [sc, hdc] in next st; rep from * across until last st, sc in last st. Ch 1, turn.

Row 126: Sc in each st across row. Change to color 1 (white) and fasten off previous color. Ch 3, turn.

Row 127: Dc in each st across row. Ch 2, turn.

Row 128: Dc in same st as ch 2, *FPdc around next st, dc in next st; rep from * across row, ending with a dc in last st. Ch 2, turn.

Row 129: Dc in same st as ch 2, *BPdc around FPdc from previous row, dc in next st; rep from * across row, ending with a dc in last st. Fasten off and weave in all yarn tails.

Flower Bookmark

Skill Level

EASY

Materials

 MEDIUM 4 less than 15 yards

Hook: 3.5 mm/U.S. E-4
Other: Tapestry needle

Stitches Used

Chain stitch (ch)
Double crochet (dc)
Half double crochet (hdc)
Magic circle
Single crochet (sc)
Slip stitch (sl st)

Tip: The finished bookmark is about 14" long from end to end.

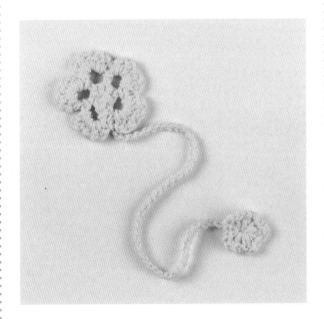

Instructions

Large Flower

Make a magic circle.

Round 1: 5 sc in magic circle. Sl st in first sc to close round.

Round 2: Ch 1, sc in same st as initial ch 1, *(ch 4, sc in next st); rep from * around. Sl st in first sc to close round.

Round 3: *Sl st in ch-4 sp, *working in same ch-4 sp:* (ch 1, 2 dc, hdc, 2 dc, ch 1, sl st); rep from * around. Sl st in first sl st to close round.

Ch 55 for stem. Add or subtract chains for a longer or shorter bookmark.

Small Flower

Sl st in 4th ch from hook to create a ring.

Round 1: *Working into the ring:* *(ch 1, dc, ch 1, sc); rep from * 5 times. Sl st in first ch 1 to close. Fasten off and weave in all yarn tails.

Coasters

Skill Level

■■□□ **EASY**

Materials

 Cotton yarn in 2 colors (less than 120 yards of each)

Hook: 5.5 mm/U.S. I-9
Other: Tapestry needle

Stitches Used

Chain stitch (ch)
Magic circle
Single crochet (sc)
Single crochet increase (sc inc)
Slip stitch (sl st)

Tip: **How to sc increase:** Work a single crochet in next stitch of previous round. Work another single crochet in that same stitch to complete the sc inc.

Instructions

Using main color (here in gray), make a magic circle.

Round 1: 6 sc in magic circle. Join with a sl st in first sc.

Round 2: Ch 1, sc inc in each sc around. Join with a sl st in first sc.

Change to contrast color (here in light green).

Round 3: Ch 1, sc inc in each sc around. Join with a sl st in first sc.

Round 4: Ch 1, *(sc, ch 1, sc) in next sc, skip next st; repeat from * around. Join with a sl st in first sc.

Round 5: Ch 1, *(sc, ch 1, sc) in ch-1 sp; repeat from * around. Join with a sl st in first sc.

Change to main color (gray).

Round 6: Ch 1, *4 sc in ch-1 sp; repeat from * around. Join with a sl st in first sc.

Fasten off and weave in yarn tails.

Repeat to make additional coasters. You can make all coasters using the same main color and contrast color, or mix it up by swapping the 2 colors for some.

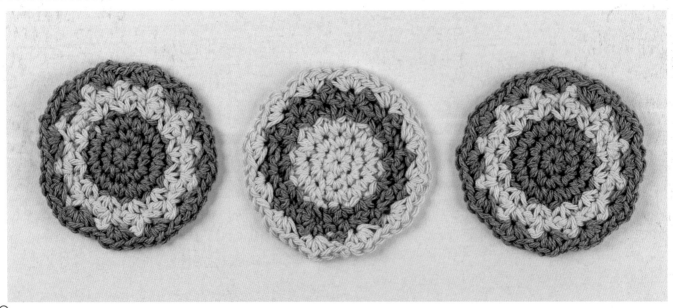

Crochet Shrug

Skill Level

EASY

Materials

 900 yards

Hook: 8 mm/U.S. L-11
Other: Tapestry needle

Stitches Used

Chain stitch (ch)

Half double crochet (hdc)

Single crochet (sc)

Whipstitch

Instructions

Ch 100.

Row 1: Hdc in 3rd ch from hook and in each ch st across row. Ch 1, turn.

Rows 2–4: Hdc in each st across row. Ch 1, turn.

Row 5: *(Sc, ch 1, sc) in next st, sk next st; rep from * across until last st. Sc in last st. Ch 1, turn.

Rows 6–65: *(Sc, ch 1, sc) in next ch-1 sp; rep from * across until last st. Sc in last st. Ch 1, turn.

Row 66: *Hdc in next ch-1 sp, sk next sc, hdc in next sc; rep from * across row. Ch 1, turn.

Rows 67–70: Hdc in each st across row. Ch 1, turn. After final row, fasten off and weave in yarn tails.

whipstitched seam

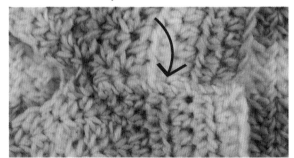

Finishing

You will now have a rectangle that is roughly 40" wide and 27" tall. Lay out rectangle and fold in each corner halfway to meet the other evenly. Leave an opening 9" across for each arm hole. Using matching yarn and a tapestry needle, whipstitch (see pages 72–73) remaining seam where short ends meet to create arm holes on both sides. Weave in all yarn tails when done.

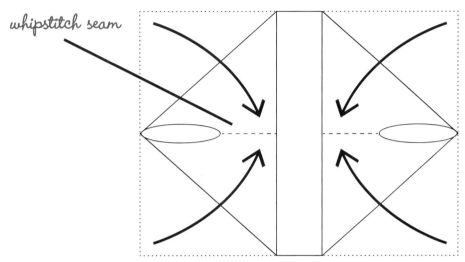

whipstitch seam

leave a 9" opening for each arm hole

Round Basket

Stitches Used

Chain stitch (ch)

Magic circle

Single crochet (sc)

Single crochet in back loop only (sc blo)

Single crochet increase (sc inc)

Single crochet spike stitch (sc spike st)

Slip stitch (sl st)

Skill Level

☐☐☐☐☐
EASY

Materials

MEDIUM 4
360 yards of main color,
120 yards of border color

Hook: 5 mm/U.S. H-8
Other: Tapestry needle

Tip: The finished basket is about 10" across and 6" high.

Instructions

Work entire pattern using 2 strands of yarn held together at the same time, treating the 2 strands as 1 strand.

Using main color (here in tan), make a magic circle.

Round 1: 6 sc in magic circle. Sl st in top of first sc to close round.

Round 2: Ch 1, sc inc in each st around. Sl st in top of first sc to close.

Round 3: Ch 1, *sc, sc inc; rep from * around. Sl st in top of first sc to close.

Round 4: Ch 1, *2 sc, sc inc; rep from * around. Sl st in top of first sc to close.

Round 5: Ch 1, *3 sc, sc inc; rep from * around. Sl st in top of first sc to close.

Round 6: Ch 1, *4 sc, sc inc; rep from * around. Sl st in top of first sc to close.

Round 7: Ch 1, *5 sc, sc inc; rep from * around. Sl st in top of first sc to close.

Round 8: Ch 1, *6 sc, sc inc; rep from * around. Sl st in top of first sc to close.

Round 9: Ch 1, *7 sc, sc inc; rep from * around. Sl st in top of first sc to close.

Round 10: Ch 1, *8 sc, sc inc; rep from * around. Sl st in top of first sc to close.

Round 11: Ch 1, *9 sc, sc inc; rep from * around. Sl st in top of first sc to close.

Round 12: Ch 1, *10 sc, sc inc; rep from * around. Sl st in top of first sc to close.

Round 13: Ch 1, sc in each st around. Sl st in top of first sc to close.

Round 14: Ch 1, sc blo in each st around. Sl st in top of first sc to close.

Rounds 15–28: Ch 1, sc in each st around. Sl st in top of first sc to close.

Change to border color (here in blue).

Round 29: Ch 1, *sc spike st in next st, sc in next st; rep from * around. Sl st in top of first sc to close.

Round 30: Ch 1, *sc in next st, sc spike st in next st; rep from * around. Sl st in top of first sc to close.

Round 31: Repeat round 29.

Round 32: Repeat round 30.

Round 33: Sl st in each st around. Sl st in first sl st to close.

Fasten off and weave in yarn tails.

Tip: **Sc spike stitch:** Instead of inserting hook under top loops of next stitch, insert hook into space directly below next stitch 1 round down. Yo, draw yarn through stitch. Pull resulting loop up to height of current round. Yo, draw yarn through both loops on hook to complete a sc spike st. Note: Because pattern is worked holding 2 strands of yarn together, each yo and resulting loop on hook will contain 2 strands. Treat each 2-loop set as 1 loop regardless of stitch.

sc spike stitch border

Donut with Sprinkles

Skill Level

EASY

Materials

 MEDIUM 4 in 2 colors (120 yards of each), plus colorful yarn scraps for sprinkles

Hook: 3.5 mm/U.S. E-4
Other: Polyfill stuffing, stitch marker, tapestry needle

Stitches Used

Chain stitch (ch)
Single crochet (sc)
Single crochet increase (sc inc)
Slip stitch (sl st)
Whipstitch

Instructions

The donut will be worked in 2 pieces, the top frosting half (here in white) and the bottom cake half (here in tan).

Place a stitch marker in the first stitch of each new round and move it up as you work.

Start with the frosting color (white). Ch 25.

Round 1: Sl st in first ch st to form a ring. *Sc inc, sc; rep from * around until last st, sc inc in last st.

Round 2: *7 sc, sc inc; rep from * around until last 6 sts. 6 sc in each of the remaining 6 sts.

Round 3: *5 sc, sc inc; rep from * around.

Round 4: *6 sc, sc inc; rep from * around.

Round 5: *7 sc, sc inc; rep from * around.

Round 6: *8 sc, sc inc; rep from * around.

Rounds 7–10: Sc in each st around.

Fasten off, leaving a long 12" tail to sew donut together.

Repeat the pattern with the cake color (here in tan) but do not leave a long tail for sewing. Instead, fasten off and weave in tails once finished with round 10.

Finishing

Once both sides of donut are complete, hold donut halves with wrong sides facing together. Using a new 10" length of tan yarn, whipstitch inner circle of donut halves together (see pages 72–73 for whipstitch instructions). Weave in yarn tail once complete.

Using a tapestry needle and scraps of colorful yarn, sew sprinkles of varying sizes on frosting (white) half of donut, starting from wrong side and working out.

Finally, using 12" tail left from frosting half of donut, begin whipstitching outer edges of 2 donut halves together, wrong sides together and right sides facing out, and stuffing with polyfill as you go. Make sure to stuff firmly to evenly fill donut. Weave in tail once complete.

Baby Booties

Skill Level

EASY

Materials

 Cotton yarn, 120 yards

Hook: 3.5 mm/U.S. E-4
Other: Tapestry needle

Stitches Used

Chain stitch (ch)
Double crochet 2 together (dc2tog)
Half double crochet (hdc)
Half double crochet in back loop only (hdc blo)
Half double crochet increase (hdc inc)
Single crochet (sc)
Single crochet 2 together (sc2tog)
Slip stitch (sl st)

Tip: These booties are intended for newborns. For larger or smaller booties, increase or decrease the hook size. Finished booties are about 3" high; soles are nearly 4" long.

Instructions

Sole

Ch 10.

Round 1: Sc in 2nd ch from hook and each of next 7 sts. 5 sc in the last ch, continue working on other side of chain and work 1 sc in each of next 7 sts until last st, work 2 sc in last st. Sl st in first sc to join.

Round 2: Ch 2, hdc in same st as ch 2, 7 hdc, hdc inc in each of next 5 sts, 7 hdc, hdc inc in each of last 2 sts. Sl st in top of ch 2 to join.

Round 3: Ch 2, hdc in same st as ch 2, 12 hdc, hdc inc in each of next 3 sts, 12 hdc, hdc inc in each of last 2 sts. Sl st in top of ch 2 to join.

Sides

Rounds 4–5: Ch 2, hdc blo in each st around. Sl st in top of ch 2 to join.

Toe and Foot Top

Round 6: Ch 2, 11 hdc, [dc2tog] 6 times, 12 hdc. Sl st in top of ch 2 to join.

Round 7: Ch 2, 10 hdc, [dc2tog] 4 times, 11 hdc. Sl st in top of ch 2 to join.

Tip: Dc2tog: Yo, insert hk in next st, yo, draw through st (3 lps on hk), yo, draw through first 2 lps on hk (2 lps left on hk), yo, insert hk in next st, yo, draw through st (4 lps on hk), yo, draw through first 2 lps on hk (3 lps on hk), yo, draw through all 3 lps on hk.

Ankle

Round 8: Ch 1, 11 sc, [sc2tog] 2 times, 10 sc. Sl st in top of first sc to join.

Rounds 9–11: Ch 2, hdc in each st around. Sl st in top of ch 2 to join.

Round 12: Ch 1, sc in each st around. Sl st in first sc to join. Fasten off and weave in yarn tails.

Repeat to make the 2nd bootie.

Catnip Fish Toy

Skill Level

EASY

Materials

 Cotton yarn, less than 30 yards

Hook: 3.5 mm/U.S. E-4

Other: Catnip, polyfill stuffing, stitch marker, tapestry needle

Stitches Used

Chain stitch (ch)
Double crochet (dc)
Half double crochet (hdc)
Magic circle
Single crochet (sc)
Single crochet 2 together (sc2tog)
Single crochet increase (sc inc)
Slip stitch (sl st)
Treble crochet (tr)

Instructions

Place a stitch marker in first stitch of each round and move it up as you work.

Make a magic circle.

Round 1: 6 sc in magic circle.

Round 2: Sc inc in each st around.

Round 3: *Sc inc, sc; rep from * around.

Rounds 4–5: Sc in each st around.

Round 6: *Sc inc, 2 sc; rep from * around.

Round 7: Sc in each st around.

Round 8: *Sc inc, 3 sc; rep from * around.

Round 9: Sc in each st around.

Round 10: *Sc2tog, 3 sc; rep from * around.

Round 11: Sc in each st around.

Round 12: *Sc2tog, 2 sc; rep from * around.

Rounds 13–14: Sc in each st around.

Round 15: *Sc2tog, sc; rep from * around.

Round 16: Sc in each st around, sl st in first sc to join. Do not fasten off.

Stuff the fish with polyfill and catnip.

Tip: Add catnip to a zippered bag of polyfill and let them sit together for a while. The polyfill will take on the scent of the catnip and it won't be as messy as trying to fill the fish with loose catnip!

Round 17: Ch 1, *6 sc, ch 1; rep from * around. Sl st in top of first sc to join.

Pinch the last round together, creating a straight line. For row 18, you will be working through 2 corresponding stitches at the same time, one from each side pinched together. This row will close off the opening of the fish, creating the tail.

Row 18: Ch 3, *working through 2 corresponding stitches, one from each side pinched together:* 3 tr in next st, (tr, dc) in next st, (dc, hdc) in next st, (hdc, dc) in next st, (dc, tr) in next st, 3 tr in next st, ch 3 and sl st in same space as last tr.

Fasten off and weave in yarn tails.

Bear Diaper Cover & Hat

Skill Level

EASY

Materials

 218 yards of main color, less than 25 yards of contrast color

Hook: 5 mm/U.S. H-8
Other: 2 small buttons for eyes, 5/8-inch button for diaper cover, 1½-inch pom-pom maker, scissors, tapestry needle

Stitches Used

Chain stitch (ch)
Double crochet (dc)
Double crochet increase (dc inc)
Half double crochet (hdc)
Half double crochet increase (hdc inc)
Magic circle
Single crochet (sc)
Single crochet increase (sc inc)
Slip stitch (sl st)

Tip: This diaper cover and hat are intended for newborns. To make the set larger or smaller, increase or decrease the crochet hook size.

Instructions

The diaper cover pattern starts with a rectangular center panel that will fold up in front, then continues with a wider triangular section that will cover baby's backside. The buttonholes on the triangular section in back will wrap around baby's sides and fasten together with one button on the center panel in front.

Diaper Cover

Using main color (here in brown), ch 15.

Row 1: Dc in 3rd ch from hook, dc in each ch st across row.

Rows 2–9: Ch 3 (counts as first dc), dc in each st across row. Turn.

Rows 10–13: Ch 3 (counts as first dc), 2 dc in same st as ch 3, dc in each st across row until last st, 3 dc in last st. Turn.

Rows 14–18: Ch 3 (counts as first dc), dc in same st as ch 3, dc in each st across row until last st, 2 dc in last st. Turn.

Row 19: Ch 7, sl st in 5th ch from hook to form a loop, dc in same st, dc in each st across until last st, 2 dc in last st, ch 5, sl st in first ch you made of ch 5 to form a loop. Turn.

Row 20: Ch 3 (counts as first dc), sl st to bottom of previous row, 8 dc into ch-5 loop, dc in each st across, 8 dc into ch-5 loop. Sl st to bottom of previous row. Do not turn or fasten off. Continue using main color (brown) yarn to work border.

Border

Working in ends of rows along first angled edge, 3 sc into the side of each dc. For the first straight edge of center panel, alternate between 2 sc and 3 sc into the side of each dc. Use 3 sc to turn the corner. Work 1 sc in each st of bottom row of center panel. Use 3 sc to turn the corner. For 2nd straight edge of center panel, alternate between 2 sc and 3 sc into the side of each dc. For 2nd angled edge, work 3 sc into the side of each dc. When you reach first buttonhole, work 2 sc in each dc of the ch-5 loop. Work 1 sc in each dc across long top edge. Finish by working 2 sc in each dc of the other ch-5 loop (2nd buttonhole). Fasten off and weave in yarn tails.

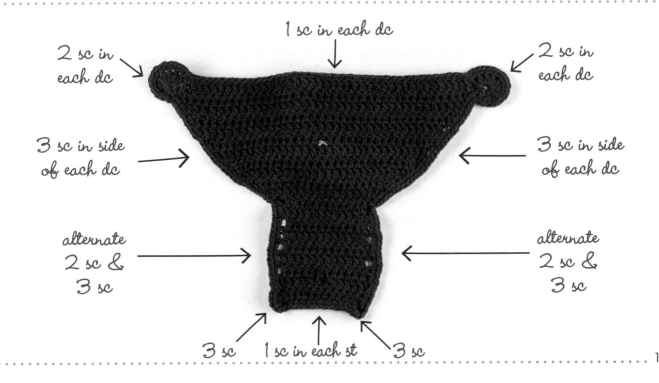

On right side of diaper cover, halfway across bottom of center panel, sew the 5/8-inch button between first and second row of dc using a length of brown yarn and a tapestry needle.

Tip: The finished diaper cover has a 13" circumference around waist and is about 5" high when buttoned.

Tail

Using approximately 160" of tan yarn and a 1½-inch pom-pom maker, create a pom-pom for the tail (see pages 69–71 for pom-pom instructions). Sew the pom-pom tail onto the back of the diaper cover using a tapestry needle.

Tip: **Dc increase:** Work a double crochet in next stitch. Work another double crochet in that same stitch to complete the dc inc.

Hat

Using main color (brown) yarn, make a magic circle.

Round 1: Ch 3 (counts as dc), 11 dc in the magic circle. Sl st in top of ch 3 to join.

Round 2: Ch 2, dc inc in each st around. Sl st in top of first dc to join.

Round 3: Ch 2, *dc inc, dc; rep from * around. Sl st in top of first dc to join.

Round 4: Ch 2, *dc inc, 2 sc; rep from * around. Sl st in top of first dc to join.

Rounds 5–10: Ch 2, dc in each st around. Sl st in top of first dc to join.

Round 11: Ch 1, sc in each st around. Sl st in top of first sc to join. Fasten off and weave in tails.

Tip: **Hdc increase:** Work an hdc in next stitch. Work another hdc in that same stitch to complete the hdc inc.

Ears (make 2)

Starting with contrast color (tan) yarn for each ear, make a magic circle.

Round 1: 8 hdc in the magic circle. Sl st in top of first hdc to join.

Round 2: Hdc inc in each st around. Sl st in top of first hdc to join.

Change to main color (brown) yarn.

Round 3: Sc in each st around. Fasten off, leaving a 6" tail for sewing ears onto hat.

Sew ears to sides on top of hat, approximately around rounds 3 and 4.

Muzzle

Starting with main color (brown) yarn, make a magic circle.

Round 1: 6 sc in the magic circle. Sl st in top of first sc to join.

Change to contrast color (tan) yarn.

Round 2: Sc inc in each st around. Sl st in top of first sc to join.

Round 3: *Sc, sc inc; rep from * around. Sl st in top of first sc to join. Fasten off, leaving a 12" tail for sewing.

Using 12" tail, sew muzzle onto front of hat, close to bottom and in center, approximately covering rounds 7–10.

Sew buttons for eyes onto hat on either side of muzzle, approximately on round 7, using matching yarn and a tapestry needle. Weave in all yarn tails.

Tip: The finished hat has a circumference of about 14" at the brim.

Cactus

Skill Level

EASY

Materials

 120 yards of brown, 120 yards of green, plus scraps of pink for flowers

Hook: 3.5 mm/U.S. E-4
Other: Polyfill stuffing, stitch marker, tapestry needle

Stitches Used

Chain stitch (ch)
Double crochet (dc)
Magic circle
Single crochet (sc)
Single crochet 2 together (sc2tog)
Single crochet in back loop only (sc blo)
Single crochet increase (sc inc)
Slip stitch (sl st)
Treble crochet (tr)
Whipstitch

Instructions

Place a stitch marker in the first stitch of each round and move it up as you work.

Soil

Using brown yarn, make a magic circle.

Round 1: 6 sc in the magic circle.

Round 2: Sc inc in each st around.

Round 3: *Sc, sc inc; repeat from * around.

Round 4: *2 sc, sc inc; repeat from * around.

Round 5: *3 sc, sc inc; repeat from * around.

Round 6: *4 sc, sc inc; repeat from * around.

Rounds 7–15: Sc in each st around.

Round 16: *4 sc, sc2tog; repeat from * around.

Round 17: *3 sc, sc2tog; repeat from * around.

Round 18: *2 sc, sc2tog; repeat from * around.

Stuff generously with polyfill.

Round 19: *Sc, sc2tog; repeat from * around.

Round 20: *Sc2tog; repeat from * around.

Fasten off and weave in yarn tails.

Tip: The completed cactus fits perfectly in a small flower pot or bowl and never needs watering!

Cactus

Using green yarn, ch 16.

Row 1: Sc in 2nd ch from hook, sc in each ch st across row. Ch 1, turn.

Rows 2–24 (or until rectangle is 5.5" across): Sc blo in each st across row. Ch 1, turn.

Fasten off, leaving a long 20" tail after last row for the drawstring closure on the top, the whipstitch seam along the side, and the drawstring closure on the bottom of the cactus.

First, thread the 20" tail through a tapestry needle. Working along the long edge of the rectangle, sew through the top sides (loops) of the stitches along edge, pulling as you go like a drawstring. This creates the closed top of the cactus.

Next, join the short edges of the rectangle together with a whipstitch (see pages 72–73), working through both layers. Now only the bottom of the cactus will be open. Stuff generously with polyfill.

Finally, work the same drawstring closure you used for the top of the cactus along the bottom edge of the cactus, pulling closed as you go.

Once complete, use the same tail to sew the cactus to the soil, attaching it on all sides, all the way around.

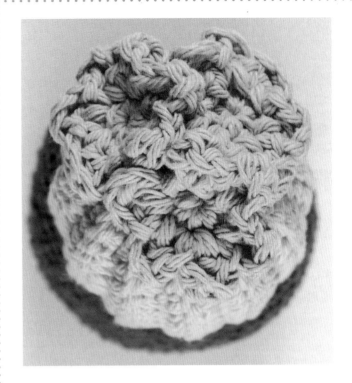

Flowers (make 3)

Using scraps of pink yarn, make a magic circle.

Round 1: 6 sc in the magic circle.

Round 2: Sl st to first sc. *In the same st you did the sl st in* [ch 2, tr, dc], *sl st in next st, in same st you did the sl st in* [ch 2, tr, dc]; repeat from * around. Sl st in first st to end round.

Fasten off, leaving a short tail for attaching the flower to the cactus.

Once you have completed 3 flowers, use the tails and a tapestry needle to sew them into the top of the cactus. Weave in all yarn tails.

Tip: Sc blo: Insert hook under back loop only of next stitch, then complete sc as usual: yarn over, draw yarn through first loop on hook, yarn over, draw yarn through both loops on hook to complete the sc blo.

Tip: The completed cactus is nearly 6.5" from top of flowers to the bottom of soil base. The soil has a circumference of about 9" around the base and is about 3" high.